WORLD GEOGRAPHY AND YOU

The Complete Edition

ABOUT THE AUTHOR

Vivian Bernstein has been a teacher in the New York Public School System for a number of years. She received her Master of Arts degree from New York University. Bernstein is the author of *World History and You, America's Story,* and *Health and You,* also for Steck-Vaughn Company.

ACKNOWLEDGMENTS

McNee/Tom Stack & Associates; 67—© Don Rutledge/Tom Stack & Associates; 68—© Courtesy of Union Carbide Corporation; 72, 74—© Terry Pommett/INSTOCK; 81—© James E. Staples/INSTOCK; 82—© Owen Franken/Stock, Boston; 88—© Spencer Swanger/Tom Stack & Associates; 90—© M. Timothy O'Keefe/Tom Stack & Associates; 96—© Anestis Diakopoulos/Stock, Boston; 97—© Cary Wolinsky/Stock, Boston; 98—© Owen Franken/Stock, Boston; 99—© Peter Menzel/Stock, Boston; 105—UPI/Bettmann Newsphotos; 106—© Owen Franken/Stock, Boston; 112—Courtesy Belgian National Tourist Office; 114—UPI/Bettmann Newsphotos; 115—© D. and J. Heaton/Stock, Boston; 119, 120, 121—EASTFOTO; 126, 128—Tass from SOVFOTO; 132—© 1985 Ardella Reed; 134—© M. Gilson/Tom Stack & Associates; 139, 140—AP/Wide World Photos; 142, 146, 148—UPI/Bettmann Newsphotos; 155—© Tim Carlson/Stock, Boston; 156—© Owen Franken/Stock, Boston; 157—© Mickey Gibson/Tom Stack & Associates; 163—© Owen Franken/Stock, Boston; 164—Courtesy Egyptian State Tourist Administration; 165—© M. Timothy O'Keefe/Tom Stack & Associates; 171—© Owen Franken/Stock, Boston; 172—© John Running/Stock, Boston; 177—© George Bellerose/Stock, Boston; 179, 180, 185—© Owen Franken/Stock, Boston; 187—AP/Wide World Photos; 194, 200, 201—© Owen Franken/Stock, Boston; 207—© Owen Franken/Stock, Boston; 208—© Ira Kirschenbaum/Stock, Boston; 215—AP/Wide World Photos; 216—Courtesy South African Tourist Corp.; 220—© Owen Franken/Stock, Boston; 221—© Don Fawcett/Tom Stack & Associates; 222—© Owen Franken/Stock, Boston; 228—© Mickey Gibson/Tom Stack & Associates; 229—© George Bellerose/Stock, Boston; 230—© Stuart Cohen/Stock, Boston; 236—© Cary Wolinsky/Stock, Boston; 237—© Norman Prince, 1985; 238—© Jean-Claude Lejeune/Stock, Boston; 243—© Norman Prince, 1985; 245—© Jean-Claude Lejeune/Stock, Boston; 246—© Gary Milburn/Tom Stack & Associates; 251—© E. Hanumantha Rao/Tom Stack & Associates; 252—© Ulrike Welsch/Stock, Boston; 253—© Jean-Claude Lejeune/Stock, Boston; 260—© Julie Houck/Stock, Boston; 261—© Warren Garst/Stock, Boston; 267—© Ira Kirschenbaum/Stock, Boston; 269—© Gary Stallings/Tom Stack & Associates; 273—AP/Wide World Photos; 275—© Gary Stallings/Tom Stack & Associates; 280—© Diane M. Lowe/Stock, Boston; 281—© J.R. Holland/Stock, Boston; 282—© Hayman Michael/Stock, Boston; 289—© Bill Noel Kleeman/Tom Stack & Associates; 293—© Mickey Gibson/Tom Stack & Associates; 294—© Sheryl S. McNee/Tom Stack & Associates.

ISBN   0-8114-1581-3

1 2 3 4 5 6 7 8 9 0 VP 92 91 90 89 88

Steck-Vaughn

WORLD GEOGRAPHY AND YOU

The Complete Edition

Vivian Bernstein

Steck-Vaughn
Company

A Subsidiary of National Education Corporation

Table of Contents

PART 1:

United States
Canada
Latin America
Europe

UNIT ONE

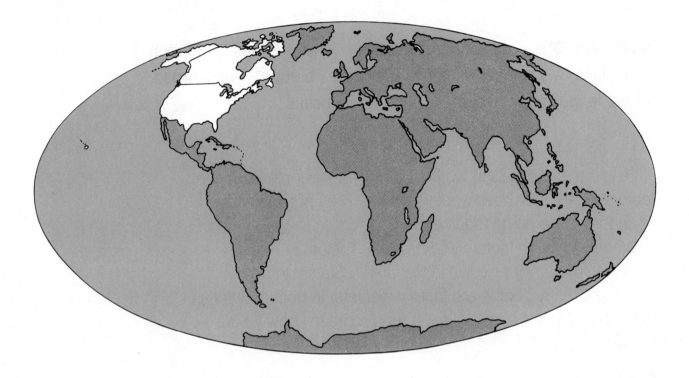

The United States and Canada

You will read these chapters in Unit 1:

CHAPTER 1

Two Countries of North America

NEW WORDS: factory   Canada   United States   French Canadians   Quebec   North America   border   unguarded official languages   south   north   industrial

It is the end of a long working day. Three people leave the factory where they have worked all day. They get into a car. Then they drive home together.

Where do these factory workers live? They may live in Canada. They may also live in the United States. In both countries, many people are factory workers. In both countries, many people own cars. We must read more to know where the workers live.

Sign in French and English at the Canadian border

At last the driver comes to the street where she lives. The street has a French name. The driver parks the car. She says good-bye to the other workers in French. They answer in French. Then they walk to their own homes. Each person is carrying a French newspaper.

In which country do these workers live? They are from Canada. They are French Canadians. They live in Quebec. Most people in Quebec speak French. In the rest of Canada, most people speak English.

The United States and Canada are the two largest countries of North America. Canada is the second largest country in the world. The United States is the world's fourth largest country.

THE UNITED STATES AND CANADA

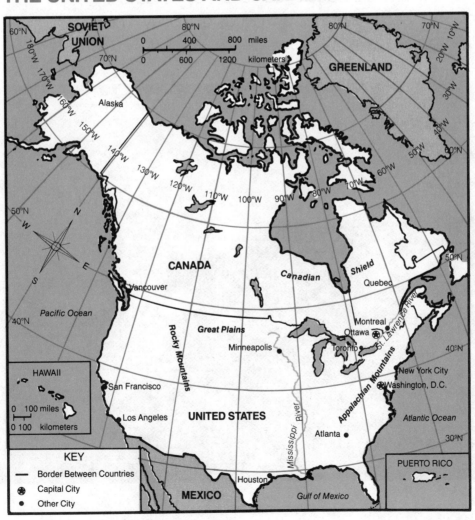

A long border separates the United States from Canada. It is the world's longest unguarded border. The two countries are friendly. People of both countries often cross the border to visit each other.

How are the United States and Canada different from each other? Canada has two official languages. English and French are the languages of Canada. The United States has one official language. English is the official language of the United States.

The United States has ten times more people than Canada. People live in the south and in the north of the United States. Northern Canada is always very cold. Few people live in northern Canada. Most Canadians live in the south.

The two countries are different in other ways. They have different laws and different leaders. Some of their holidays are different. They each have their own kinds of money. They also have their own flags.

A dairy farm in Minnesota

How are the United States and Canada alike? Both countries have many large cities. Most people live in cities. The United States and Canada have excellent farm land. Both countries grow far more food than they need for their own people. The two countries sell food to other countries of the world.

The United States and Canada are both industrial countries. Industrial countries have many factories. Paper and clothing are made in the factories of Canada and the United States. Cars, trucks, and other goods are made in their factories. Both countries sell many of the goods they make to other countries of the world.

Schools are important in both countries. Children must spend many years in school. In both countries, almost everyone knows how to read and write.

The United States and Canada are rich countries. They are alike in many ways. They are different in many ways. In the next chapters, you will learn more about the United States and Canada.

Think, Remember, Write

A. Find the Answer

The United States and Canada are alike in many ways. On your paper, copy each sentence that tells how they are alike. You should write 5 sentences.

1. Both countries have two official languages.

2. In both countries, most people live in cities.

3. Both countries have few people in the south.

4. Both countries make cars in factories.

5. The United States and Canada are industrial countries.

6. Both countries have the same money.

7. Both countries have the same flag.

8. Both countries grow a lot of food.

9. In both countries, children spend many years in school.

B. Finish Up

Finish each sentence with the words **the United States** or **Canada.**

1. Many people live in the north and in the south of _____.

2. _____ is the second largest country in the world.

3. The world's fourth largest country is _____.

4. English and French are the official languages of _____.

5. Few people live in northern _____.

6. Quebec is one part of _____ where most people speak French.

C. Write It Right

The words in the sentences below are mixed up. Write each sentence correctly.

1. French Canadians Quebec. Most in live

2. always cold. is Canada Northern

3. larger than Canada is States. United the

4. States United The Canada. than more people ten times has

5. official language United States. English of the the is

Skill Words

earth   spaceship   globe   model

Where do you live? Do you live in a city or in a town? Your city or town is part of a country. Every country of the world is on the earth. The earth is every person's home.

Look at the picture of the earth on this page. This picture was taken from a spaceship. The earth is round like a ball. It has land and water. The earth is very, very big.

A globe is a model of the earth. This means a globe is a small copy of the earth. A globe is round like the earth.

You can see oceans and land on a globe. You can see the countries of the world. Can you find Canada on a globe? Where is the United States on a globe? Find the Pacific Ocean. Globes help us learn about the earth.

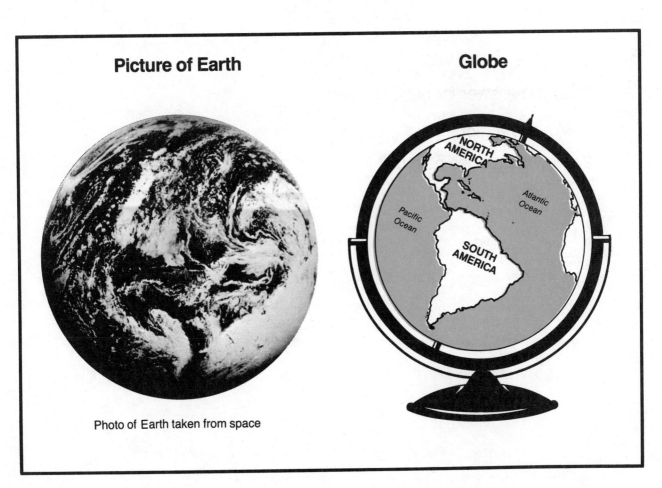

Picture of Earth

Photo of Earth taken from space

Globe

NORTH AMERICA

Pacific Ocean

Atlantic Ocean

SOUTH AMERICA

A. Finish Up

Use the words in dark print to finish each sentence. Write the words you choose on your paper.

oceans   **round**   **model**
globe   **earth**

1. The earth is _____ like a ball.

2. Every person's home is on the _____.

3. A globe is a _____ of the earth.

4. You can see _____ on a globe.

5. You can see the many countries of the world on a _____.

B. Write the Answer

Write the answer for each question.

1. What is a globe?

2. How do globes help us?

CHAPTER 2

The United States: An Interesting Land

NEW WORDS: Americans   Alaska   Hawaii   island
Puerto Rico   Atlantic Ocean   east   Pacific Ocean   west
deserts   Great Plains   California   transportation   Mississippi River

Do you live in the north of the United States where the winters are cold? On cold winter days, people in the north can buy oranges in food stores. These oranges grew on trees that were far from home. Orange trees grow where the weather is always warm. Every day people buy many kinds of food that come from faraway states. How does food from faraway states get to your home? You will soon find the answers.

Oranges and other fruits at a grocery store

The United States is a very big country. It is made up of 50 states. The people of all 50 states are called Americans. Alaska and Hawaii are two states that are far from all the other states. Alaska is near northern Canada. Many parts of Alaska are very cold throughout the year. The state of Hawaii is a group of islands in the Pacific Ocean. Hawaii has warm, wet weather.

Puerto Rico is an island that belongs to the United States. The people of Puerto Rico are Americans. English and Spanish are the languages of Puerto Rico.

The United States is between two oceans. The Atlantic Ocean is to the east of the United States. The Pacific Ocean is to the west.

THE UNITED STATES

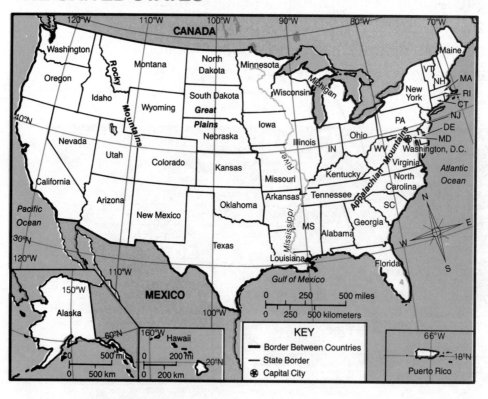

There are mountains in the west and in the east of the United States. The mountains in the west are very tall and rocky. The mountains in the east are lower and smoother.

Some of the western states have deserts. A desert is a hot

land with little rain. There are few plants, trees, or animals. Not many Americans live in the deserts.

The United States has a lot of good farm land. Part of the land between the eastern and western mountains is called the Great Plains. Many farms are on the Great Plains. Corn and wheat are grown on the Great Plains. Wheat is used to make bread and flour. It is an important food. Most of our bread is made from wheat grown on the Great Plains.

Farms on the Great Plains

Other parts of the country also have good farm land. The southern states have warmer winters than the northern states. There are many farms in the southern states. Parts of the state of California also have warm winters. A lot of food also comes from California. Many foods can grow in the southern states and in California that cannot grow in the north.

The United States has very good transportation. Airplanes carry goods and people to all parts of the country. Railroads carry people, food, and other goods to many states. The United States has many wide highways. Cars, trucks, and buses travel across the country. How do you think oranges from the south get to the north?

The United States has many large rivers. The Mississippi is the longest river. It is one of the longest rivers in the world. It flows from the north to the south of the United States. Many shorter rivers flow into the Mississippi. The rivers are used for transportation. River ships carry goods from one part of the country to another. Farmers use the rivers too. Some places do not get enough rain. Farmers use river water to water their fields. Then crops can grow.

Many people believe that the United States is a good place to live. In the next chapter, you will learn why the United States is a leading country in the world today.

A barge on the Mississippi River

Think, Remember, Write

A. Match Up

Answer each question in Group A with an item from Group B. Write the letter of the correct answer on your paper.

<u>Group A</u>

1. Which two states are far from all the other states?

2. Which ocean is to the east of the United States?

3. What foods are grown on the Great Plains?

4. What foods are made from wheat?

5. Which states have cold winters?

<u>Group B</u>

a. corn and wheat

b. the northern states

c. bread and flour

d. Alaska and Hawaii

e. Atlantic Ocean

B. True or False

Write **T** for each sentence that is true. Write **F** for each sentence that is false, or not true.

1. The United States has 50 states.

2. Parts of Alaska are always cold.

3. English and French are the languages of Puerto Rico.

4. There are mountains in the east and west of the United States.

5. Part of the land between the eastern and western mountains is called the Great Plains.

6. There are many farms in the southern states.

7. The Mississippi River flows from the east to the west.

8. Farmers use river water to water their fields.

9. All of California is very cold during the winter.

10. People can travel across the United States on wide highways.

C. Finish Up

Use the words in dark print to finish each sentence. Write the words you choose on your paper.

Pacific   **Alaska**   **island**   **transportation**   **California**
desert   **Hawaii**   **Southern**   **Mississippi**   **Americans**

1. _____ is a state near northern Canada.

2. Puerto Rico is an _____ that belongs to the United States.

3. Americans use cars, planes, trains, and buses for _____.

4. The _____ Ocean is to the west of the United States.

5. The state of _____ is a group of islands in the Pacific Ocean.

6. _____ states have warmer winters than northern states.

7. The people of the United States are called _____.

8. A lot of food is grown in the state of _____.

9. A _____ is a hot, dry place with little rain.

10. The _____ River is the longest river in the United States.

Skill Words

map   half   pocket

A globe is a model of the earth. Because a globe is round, you can only look at one half of a globe at a time.

Maps also help us learn about the earth. They help us learn about oceans and countries. A globe shows every part of the earth. A world map also shows every part of the earth. But other maps may show only one country. Some maps show just one city. Find the United States on a globe. Find the United States on the world map on this page.

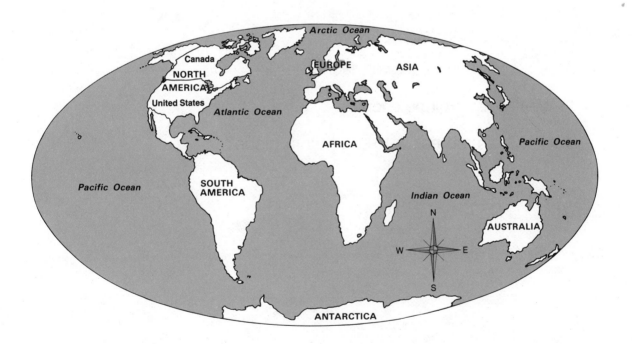

In some ways, maps are easier to use than globes. It is hard to carry a round globe with you. It is easy to carry a map. A map is flat. You can fold a map and put it in your pocket. Many books have maps in them. You will be using maps to help you learn about different countries as you read this book.

A. Finish Up

Finish each sentence with the word **globe** or **map**.

1. You can only look at one half of a _____ at a time.

2. You can see all the countries of the earth on a flat world _____.

3. A _____ may show only one country.

4. It is hard to carry a _____ with you.

5. You can fold a _____ and put it in your pocket.

B. Write the Answer

Write a sentence to answer each question.

1. What does a globe show?

2. How is a map easier to use than a globe?

CHAPTER 3

The United States: A Leading Country

NEW WORDS: vote   Election Day   government   democracy Washington, D.C.   president   natural resources   coal   iron   oil natural gas   electricity   American Indians   Europe   Africa

"**A**re you going to vote tomorrow? Which people will be good leaders for our country?" Two Americans are talking during their lunch hour. They must decide how to vote on Election Day. Every year, on Election Day, Americans vote for people to work in their government.

The government of the United States is a democracy. In a democracy, people vote for their government leaders. In a democracy, people help make laws for their government.

The government of the United States is in the city of Washington, D.C. Americans vote for people to work for them in Washington. The leader of the United States government is the president. Americans vote for a new president every four years. Every state has its own government too. Americans also vote for people to work in their state governments. The leaders of the state governments are the governors.

The United States is a leading country in the world today. Many things have made the United States a leader. American democracy makes the government strong. American farmers grow plenty of food to make Americans healthy and strong. The United States has many natural resources. These natural resources have helped the country become rich.

Natural resources are things we get from the earth. What are some of America's resources? The United States has coal and iron. It has gold and silver. Trees are a natural resource. The United States has animals and fish. It has good soil.

Electricity is produced at this dam.

Water power is another natural resource. The United States also has oil and natural gas.

How have natural resources helped the United States become a rich country? Farmers use good soil to grow food for America. The United States grows more food than any other country. Our cars, planes, buses, and trucks need oil to move. Coal, oil, natural gas, and water are used to make electricity. Americans use electricity in their homes and factories.

Factories use natural resources to make goods. Some factories make cars. Coal and iron are used in car factories. Other factories use natural resources to make big farm machines. Some factories use trees to make paper.

The United States is an industrial country. It has more factories than any other country. The United States trades with many countries of the world. It sells food to other countries. It sells factory goods. The United States does not have all the natural resources it needs. It buys oil and other resources from other countries. It buys goods from other countries. Does your family have a car? Where was it made? Perhaps it was made in another country.

22

Most Americans live in big cities. Many city people work in factories and businesses. Most Americans earn more money than people in other countries. Many people own cars. Most Americans have enough food. There are many doctors in America. Every child can go to school.

The people of America have made the country rich and strong. Who are the people of the United States? The American Indians were the first people to come to this country. Then people from Europe came to live in America. People from Africa and many other places came. People from many lands helped the United States become a great country.

Every year people from other lands come to live in the United States. Why do these people come? Many people come because they want to live in a democracy. Other people come because they are very poor. They want to have a better life in the United States.

Immigrants passing the Statue of Liberty

Farms, factories, businesses, and people have helped America become rich and strong. The United States is a leading country in the world today.

Think, Remember, Write

A. Finish Up

Use the words in dark print to finish each sentence. Write the words you choose on your paper.

**Coal   natural resources   Election Day   four   Europe
American Indians   democracy   Washington, D.C.**

1. In a _____, people vote for their government leaders.

2. Americans vote on _____.

3. The government of the United States is in _____.

4. Americans vote for a president every _____ years.

5. _____ are things we get from the earth.

6. The first people to live in America were the _____.

7. _____, oil, natural gas, and water are used to make electricity.

8. People came from _____ and Africa to live in the United States.

B. Locate the Answer

Write the correct answer to each question.

1. Who is the leader of the United States government?

   the president   the farmer   the governor

2. Which are natural resources?

   paper, books, pens   oil, iron, water power
   tables, cars, windows

3. Which goods are made in factories?

   cars and paper   air and water   oil and gold

4. Which resources are used to make electricity?

   trees, fish, gold, books   silver, animals, soil, rocks
   coal, oil, natural gas, water

5. Where do most Americans live?

   in cities   on farms   in deserts

C. Write the Answer

Write a sentence to answer each question.

1. How do Americans choose their leaders?

2. Which country has the most factories?

3. What does the United States sell to other countries?

4. What does the United States buy from other countries?

5. From where did people come to live in the United States?

6. What things have helped the United States become rich and strong?
   Write 2 sentences.

Skill Words

North Pole   South Pole   compass rose

There are four main directions. They are north, south, east, and west. When you move north, you are always moving toward the North Pole. When you move south, you are moving toward the South Pole. On most maps, north is at the top. Put your finger anywhere on a map. Move your finger to the right. You are moving east. Move your finger to the left. You are moving west.

A compass rose is used to show directions on a map. Here is a compass rose.

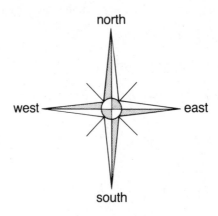

Directions on a compass rose are often shortened to N, S, E, and W. Trace the compass rose below. Write the shortened directions on it.

A. Match Up

Finish each sentence in Group A with an answer from Group B. Write the letter of the correct answer on your paper.

<table>
<tr><td>Group A</td><td>Group B</td></tr>
<tr><td>1. The four main directions are _____.</td><td>a. N, S, E, and W</td></tr>
<tr><td></td><td>b. north, south, east, and west</td></tr>
<tr><td>2. The main directions can be shortened to _____.</td><td>c. South Pole</td></tr>
<tr><td></td><td>d. compass rose</td></tr>
<tr><td>3. When you move north, you are moving toward the _____.</td><td>e. North Pole</td></tr>
<tr><td>4. When you move south, you are moving toward the _____.</td><td></td></tr>
<tr><td>5. A _____ is used to show directions on a map.</td><td></td></tr>
</table>

CHAPTER 4

Canada: Northern Giant

NEW WORDS: provinces   territories   Arctic Ocean   Canadian Shield
forests   metals   St. Lawrence River   St. Lawrence Lowlands
Toronto   Montreal   newsprint   England   prime minister
Eskimos   France

Perhaps one summer you will visit northern Canada.
Although it may be summer, the air will feel cool. People will
be wearing warm jackets. You might want to visit a big city.
You will not be able to find one. Few people live in this part of
Canada. Most of Canada's people live in warmer southern
Canada.

Canada is a very big country. It is made up of ten
provinces and two territories. The provinces are like the states
in the United States. The territories are in the far north. They
are run by the Canadian government.

The Atlantic Ocean is to the east of Canada. The Pacific

CANADA

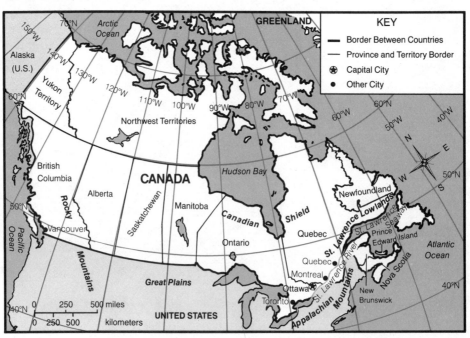

Ocean is to the west. The Arctic Ocean is to the north. The mountains in the east and west of the United States continue into Canada. The mountains in the west are very tall. Like the United States, Canada has flat land called the Great Plains. Wheat and other crops are grown on the Great Plains of southern Canada. Canada sells wheat to many countries.

Look at the map of Canada on page 28. Do you see an area called the Canadian Shield? The Canadian Shield covers nearly half of Canada. The soil of the Canadian Shield is not good for farming. The southern part of the Shield has thick forests. The northern part of the Shield is cold, icy land. Many metals can be found in this cold northern land. Not many people live in the Canadian Shield.

Large forests cover parts of the Canadian Shield.

Look at the map on page 28 again. Find the St. Lawrence River. The land around the river is called the St. Lawrence Lowlands. This is a very important part of Canada. The soil is good for farming. More than half of Canada's people live in this area. Canada's two largest cities are in the Lowlands. These cities are Toronto and Montreal. There are many factories in this area. Ships carry factory goods along the St. Lawrence River to the Atlantic Ocean. These goods are then shipped to many countries.

Toronto is a large, modern city.

Canada is very rich in natural resources. It has many forests. It has lots of animals and fish. Canada has many kinds of metals. It has iron, coal, and gold. Canada has oil. It sells oil to other countries. Canada has water power from its many rivers. Canada uses its water power to make electricity.

Canada is an industrial country. Like the United States, most people live in cities and towns. Most Canadians do not work on farms. Canadians use their natural resources in their factories.

Many goods are made in Canada's factories. Cars and trucks are made in Canada. Wood products are made from Canada's trees. Did you read a newspaper today? Newsprint is the paper used to make newspapers. The newsprint for your newspapers may have been made in Canada. Canada makes more newsprint than any other country.

Transportation is good in southern Canada. Railroads and highways join the country together in the south. There are few roads in the north. People often use airplanes to travel in northern Canada.

For many years, Canada was ruled by England. Today Canada is a free country. The queen of England is still Canada's queen. But she does not rule Canada. Canada is a democracy. People vote for their government leaders. The leader of Canada is called the prime minister.

Who are the people of Canada? The first Canadians were Eskimos and Indians. The Eskimos are people who live in the cold, icy lands of North America. Thousands of Eskimos and Indians live in Canada today. A few hundred years ago, people from England and France came to Canada. Then people from other countries in Europe came. Today there are people from every part of the world living in Canada.

Northern Canada is a cold, snowy land.

Think, Remember, Write

A. Find the Answer

On your paper, copy the sentences that tell about Canada. You should write 6 sentences.

1. The Arctic Ocean is to the south of Canada.

2. Many metals can be found in the Canadian Shield.

3. Wheat is grown on the Canadian Shield.

4. The Canadian Shield covers nearly half of Canada.

5. The two largest cities of Canada are Toronto and Montreal.

6. Toronto and Montreal are on the Great Plains of Canada.

7. More than half of Canada's people live in the St. Lawrence Lowlands.

8. Most Canadians work on farms.

9. Canada makes more newsprint than any other country.

10. Most Canadians live in towns and cities.

B. Write the Answer

Write a sentence to answer each question.

1. Where do most of the people live in Canada?

2. What are the St. Lawrence Lowlands?

3. What are some of the goods made in Canada's factories?

4. What are some of Canada's natural resources? Write 2 sentences.

5. Who were the first people to live in Canada?

C. Match Up

Finish each sentence in Group A with an answer from Group B. Write the letter of the correct answer on your paper.

Group A	Group B

Group A

1. There are railroads and highways in _____ Canada.

2. The government of Canada is a _____ .

3. Canadians _____ for their government leaders.

4. The leader of Canada is called the _____ .

5. The people who live in the cold, icy lands of North America are the _____ .

Group B

a. prime minister

b. southern

c. democracy

d. Eskimos

e. vote

SKILL BUILDER 4: Finding Directions on a Map

Skill Words

northeast   southeast   northwest   southwest

The four main directions on a map are north, south, east, and west. There are also four in-between directions. They are northeast, southeast, northwest, and southwest.

You might want to find a place on a map that is between south and east. The direction between south and east is southeast. The direction between north and east is northeast.

The compass rose shows both main and in-between directions.

Sometimes in-between directions are shortened to NE, SE, NW, and SW. Trace the compass rose below. Write the shortened in-between directions on it.

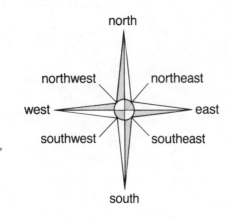

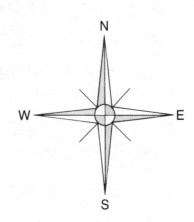

A. Finish the Sentence

Look back at the map of Canada on page 28. Then write the word that finishes the sentence.

1. Montreal is in ══ Canada.

   northwest   southwest   southeast

2. Vancouver is in ══ Canada.

   northeast   southwest   southeast

3. The Yukon Territory is in ══ Canada.

   northwest   southeast   southwest

4. The St. Lawrence River is in ══ Canada.

   southeast   northeast   northwest

CHAPTER 5

More About the United States and Canada

NEW WORDS: differences   airlines   population   one third
religions   Roman Catholics   Protestants   control   companies
polluted   acid rain   chemicals   St. Lawrence Seaway

Five hundred years ago, English and French people did not live in North America. Eskimos and Indians were the only people who lived in the United States and Canada at that time. You learned that people from Europe came to live in both countries. People from many countries of the world have made their homes in the United States and Canada. Today the United States and Canada are both industrial countries. Both countries grow more food than they need. Both countries are rich and strong.

Ships passing through the St. Lawrence Seaway

Let's look at some differences between the United States and Canada. You already learned that Canada is the larger country. The United States has ten times more people. There is good transportation all over the United States. There is little transportation in the northern part of Canada.

The government of Canada owns one of the country's railroads. It owns one of the country's airlines. It also pays doctors to care for the sick. The government of the United States does not do these things.

The government of Canada owns a railroad.

There is another big difference between the two countries. Canada has a large French population. Almost one third of the people are French Canadians. Most people in the province of Quebec are French.

The French Canadians feel proud that their families came from France. Many French Canadians do not speak English. Many English Canadians do not speak French. The two groups have different religions. Most French Canadians are Roman Catholics. Most English Canadians are Protestants. Their children often go to separate schools.

Many French Canadians are unhappy. They feel that the

English Canadians control Canada. They believe English Canadians have the best jobs. The English have more leaders in the government. They own more businesses. The French feel that the English have a better life in Canada.

Some French Canadians want Quebec to be free from the rest of Canada. They want Quebec to be a free French country. Most Canadians do not want this to happen. Quebec is a very important province. Canada cannot be a strong country without Quebec. The government is trying to find new ways to help all Canadians live together in peace.

The United States and Canada are friendly countries. Sometimes friendly countries have problems with each other. You learned that Canada has many factories. Many of these factories are owned by American companies. American companies built many Canadian factories. They control many Canadian businesses. Many Canadians do not want Americans to control their businesses.

Another worry is about polluted, or dirty, air that moves from one country to another. Polluted air can cause acid rain. Chemicals in the dirty air fall in the rain. They get into the rivers and lakes. They make the water acid. Acid rain harms plants, animals, and fish.

The United States has many factories. The factories give off chemicals which can get into the air. Many Canadians believe that their acid rain comes from American factories. They want American factories to stop polluting the air.

The United States and Canada also work together to help each other. In 1954, both countries worked together to build the St. Lawrence Seaway. This is a group of canals through rocky parts of the St. Lawrence River. Today electricity is made from the water power of the St. Lawrence Seaway. Some cities of both countries use this electricity. Large ships from both countries sail along the St. Lawrence River to the Atlantic Ocean. Then they sail on to other countries. The St. Lawrence Seaway has helped both Canada and the United States.

Canada and the United States are alike in many ways.

These ways are more important than the differences between the two countries. In the years ahead, the United States and Canada will continue to work together as friends.

Think, Remember, Write

A. Match Up

Finish each sentence in Group A with an answer from Group B. Write the letter of the correct answer on your paper.

Group A

1. Five hundred years ago, only .... lived in North America.

2. The government of .... owns an airline and a railroad.

3. Almost .... of Canada's people are French Canadians.

4. Most French Canadians are ....

5. Plants, animals, and fish are harmed by ....

Group B

a. Roman Catholics

b. acid rain

c. Canada

d. one third

e. Eskimos and Indians

B. Locate the Answer

Write the correct answer to each question.

1. Where is there little transportation?

northern Canada   northern United States   southern Canada

2. Where do most French Canadians live?

Toronto   Quebec   northern Canada

3. Which country built many factories in Canada?

England   France   the United States

4. Which two countries built the St. Lawrence Seaway together?

the United States and Canada   Canada and England

Canada and France

C. Write It Right

The words in the sentences below are mixed up. Write each sentence correctly.

1. not English. speak do Many Canadians French

2. believe French Canadians Many control English the Canada.

3. free French country. a want Quebec Canadians French Some to be

4. want Americans not do control businesses. their Canadians Many to

5. Canada and States United electricity use of the Cities Seaway. St. Lawrence from the

SKILL BUILDER 5: The Oceans of the World

Skill Words

oceans   Indian Ocean

Our earth is made of land and water. There is more water than land on the earth. Much of the earth's water is in four big oceans. The largest is the Pacific Ocean. Next in size is the Atlantic Ocean. The Indian Ocean is smaller than the Atlantic. The Arctic Ocean is the smallest ocean.

The world map on this page shows the four oceans.

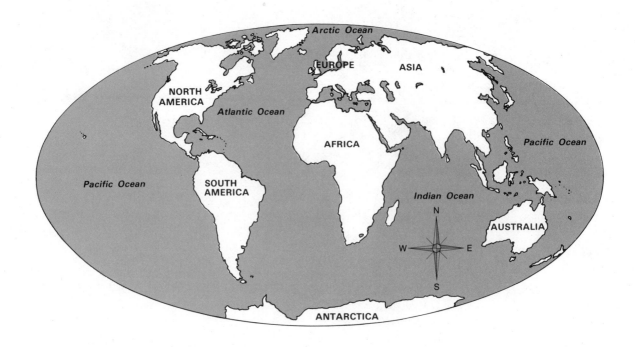

A. List It

On your paper, write the oceans in order of their size. Start with the largest ocean.

B. Mixed-up Words

The letters in the names of the oceans have been mixed up below. Rewrite the names correctly. A list of the correct words is on the right.

1. cciiaPf   Arctic

2. citrcA   Atlantic

3. tanlictA   Indian

4. dainnl   Pacific

UNIT TWO

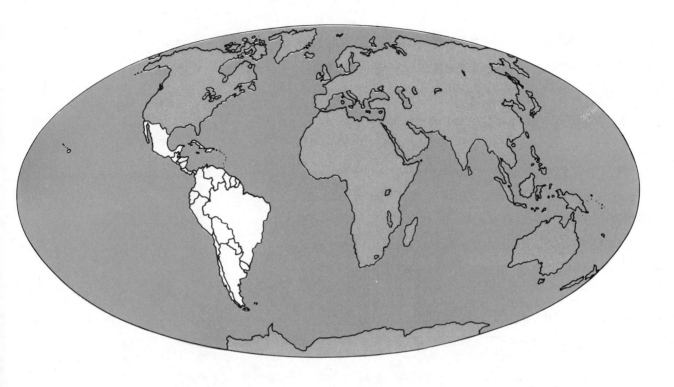

Latin America and the Caribbean

You will read these chapters in Unit 2:

CHAPTER 6

Our Southern Neighbors

NEW WORDS: Latin America   Caribbean Sea   Mexico
Central America   South America   Portugal   Spain   Brazil
Spaniards   mestizos   descent   Amazon River   rain forest
Andes Mountains   mountain chain

Every morning families in the United States eat breakfast together. They may eat bananas with their cereal. They may enjoy a chocolate drink. Parents often drink hot coffee with their breakfast.

LATIN AMERICA

What part of our breakfast comes from Latin America? Most of our coffee and bananas comes from Latin America. A lot of our sugar and chocolate is grown in Latin America too. You are probably eating some foods from Latin America every day.

All the countries to the south of the United States are called Latin America. Latin America has three parts. The small islands in the Caribbean Sea are one part. Mexico and Central America are another part. South America is the largest part of Latin America. Look at the map on page 42. Find the three parts of Latin America on the map.

Latin America has about 360 million people. Many places are very crowded. Who are the people of Latin America? The first people to live in Latin America were American Indians. About 500 years ago, people from Europe came to Latin America. These people came mostly from Portugal and Spain. People from Portugal settled in the country of Brazil. Spain ruled almost every other part of Latin America.

Many Spaniards who came to Latin America married Indian women. Their children were called mestizos. There are millions of mestizos in Latin America today. Mestizos are people of Spanish and Indian descent.

This market is in the nation of Colombia.

Blacks are another important group in Latin America. The people from Spain and Portugal brought black people from Africa to work as slaves. Today most people in the Caribbean countries are black. Europeans, Indians, mestizos, and blacks are the four large groups of people in Latin America.

The Roman Catholic religion was very important to the people who came from Spain and Portugal. They taught their religion to the Indians. Today most Latin Americans are Roman Catholics. But there are also people of other religions.

There are many large rivers in Latin America. The largest is the Amazon River. It is the second longest river in the world. It runs all the way across the country of Brazil. Many large rivers join the Amazon. The Amazon is very wide. Large ocean ships sail on the Amazon. The waters of the Amazon flow into the Atlantic Ocean.

There are many rain forests in Latin America. It rains almost every day in a rain forest. Rain forests are hot and very wet. These forests have many kinds of trees and animals. The largest rain forest in the world is near the Amazon River in Brazil.

A rain forest covers a large area of South America.

The rugged and beautiful Andes Mountains

Mountains cover a lot of land in Latin America. There are
mountains in the east and taller mountains in the west. The
tall mountains in the west of the United States continue into
Mexico. From Mexico they go into Central America and then
into South America. The islands in the Caribbean Sea have
mountains also.

The tall mountains in the west of South America are called
the Andes Mountains. The Andes go from the north to the
south of South America. The Andes are the longest mountain
chain in the world. They are much higher than the mountains
of North America. The air is always very cold at the top of the
Andes Mountains. It is so cold that many mountain tops are
always covered with snow.

Latin America has many natural resources. It has rivers and
animal life. Some countries have very good soil for farming.

Many countries are rich in metals. Some have lots of oil. These natural resources have not helped most of the people. Most Latin Americans are very poor. Many people do not have enough food to eat.

Why are there so many poor people in countries that are rich in natural resources? One reason is that many natural resources are found in the mountains and rain forests. It is hard to grow food on land covered by steep mountains. Transportation is poor in many parts of Latin America. It is hard to build roads on land covered by mountains. It is hard to build roads through hot, wet rain forests. The people cannot move natural resources from mountains and forests to factories in the cities.

There are more than 20 different countries in Latin America. Mexico and Brazil are two important Latin American countries. In the next chapters, you will learn about Mexico and Brazil. You will also learn about some of the problems of Latin America.

Think, Remember, Write

A. True or False

Write **T** for each sentence that is true. Write **F** for each sentence that is false.

1. The first Latin Americans were mestizos.

2. The Amazon River is in the country of Brazil.

3. Ocean ships can sail on the Amazon River.

4. It is cold in the rain forests of Latin America.

5. The tall mountains in the western part of South America are the Andes.

6. It is hot at the tops of the Andes Mountains.

7. Most of Latin America has very flat land.

8. Most Latin Americans are poor.

9. Many natural resources are found in the mountains and rain forests.

10. There is good transportation in every part of Latin America.

B. Finish the Story

Use the words in dark print to finish the story. Write the words you choose on your paper.

Spain   Portugal   Central   mestizos
South   blacks   Amazon River

The three parts of Latin America are the Caribbean countries, Mexico and .... America, and .... America. People from .... settled in Brazil. People from .... ruled almost all of Latin America except for Brazil. There are four large groups of people in Latin America. They are Europeans, ..., ..., and Indians. The world's second longest river is the ....

C. Write the Answer

Write a sentence to answer each question.

1. What foods do we get from Latin America?

2. What is the religion of most Latin Americans?

3. What are the four large groups of people in Latin America?

4. What is the longest mountain chain in the world?

5. Name four natural resources of Latin America.

47

SKILL BUILDER 6: The Continents of the World

Skill Words

continents   Asia   Antarctica   Australia

Our earth has very large pieces of land called continents. There are seven continents. The world map on this page shows the seven continents.

Here is a list of the seven continents in order of their size. The list starts with the largest continent.

1. Asia
2. Africa
3. North America
4. South America

5. Antarctica
6. Europe
7. Australia

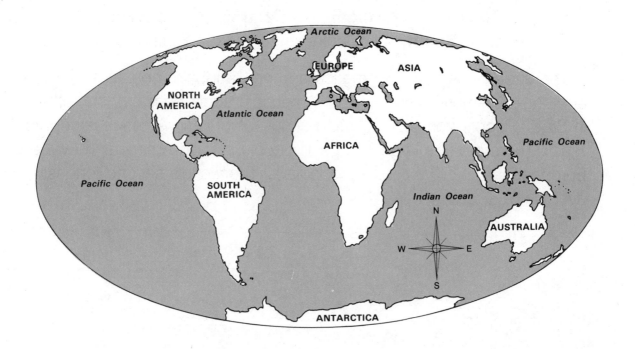

Most continents have countries on them. Canada, Mexico, and the United States are in North America. Australia is both a country and a continent. Antarctica is at the South Pole. It is the coldest continent. There are no countries on Antarctica.

A. Finish Up

Look at the list of continents again. Finish the sentence with the names of the continents in dark print.

South America   **Australia**   **Antarctica**   **Africa**

The seven continents in order of size are Asia, _____, North America, _____, _____, Europe, and _____.

B. Write the Answer

Write the answer to each question on your paper.

1. Which 3 countries are in North America?

2. Which is the largest continent?

3. Which is the smallest continent?

4. Which continent is at the South Pole?

5. Which continent is also a country?

6. Which continent has no countries?

7. What is the second largest continent?

8. Which continent is connected to North America?

CHAPTER 7

Mexico: Our Spanish Neighbor

NEW WORDS: Acapulco   Mexican   Central Plateau   plateau
sea level   Mexico City   Gulf of Mexico

It is a cold day in the northern cities of the United States. People are wearing warm coats and boots. On this same day in Mexico, thousands of people are swimming at the beach near the town of Acapulco. Every winter many people leave their cold cities and towns to visit Acapulco and other Mexican beaches. These beaches have warm weather every day of the year.

Beach and water at Acapulco, Mexico

Mexico is the country to the south of the United States. The tall mountains in the west of the United States continue into Mexico. In Mexico, the mountains form two mountain chains. One chain is in the east; the other chain is in the west. In the south, the two chains come together. The chains form a huge V-shape.

The land between the two mountain chains is called the Central Plateau. A plateau is high, flat land. The land of the Central Plateau is high above sea level. Up high the air becomes cooler. The weather in Mexico's Central Plateau is not hot. It is comfortable most days of the year.

The southern part of the Central Plateau has rich soil. The area gets plenty of rain. Farmers there grow corn and beans. Most of Mexico's cities and people are in the southern part of the Central Plateau. Mexico's largest city is there. It is called Mexico City. The northern part of the Central Plateau also has rich soil. But little rain falls on this area. Fewer people live in the north.

The Pacific Ocean is to the west of Mexico. Acapulco and other beaches are near the Pacific Ocean. The water to the

MEXICO

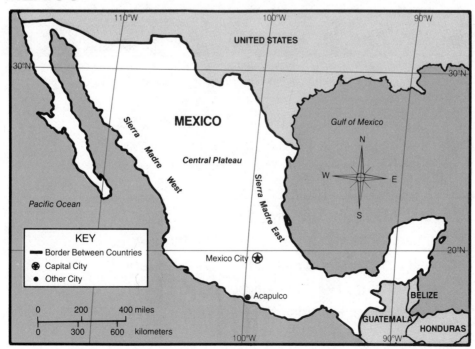

east of Mexico is called the Gulf of Mexico. There are hot rain forests near the Gulf.

Mexico has many natural resources. Iron, coal, natural gas, and silver are some resources. There are fish from the seas. There are trees from the forests. Today oil is Mexico's most important resource. Mexico is very rich in oil. It sells oil to other countries of the world.

The Mexican government owns this oil refinery.

Who are the people of Mexico? The first Mexicans were American Indians. Then people from Spain came to Mexico. There are Europeans and Indians in Mexico today. But most Mexicans are mestizos. Their families are of Spanish and Indian descent. Mexicans are proud of their Indian background. Many people can speak the Indian languages. Most people speak Spanish, and it is the official language of Mexico. Most Mexicans are Roman Catholics. Families in Mexico are generally large. Parents, children, and grandparents often live together.

Mexico's government is in Mexico City. The government is a democracy. Mexicans vote for their government leaders. The leader of the government is the president.

Mexico is a poor country today. Most of Mexico's land cannot be used for farming. Many places have too many mountains. Other parts have too little rain. In some areas, farmers are using river water to grow more food. Mexico's mountains make it hard to get to its natural resources. Mexico's population is growing very fast. Every year many babies are born. There are not enough jobs for the millions of people.

The Mexican government is working to help the poor. How are Mexicans trying to make their country a better place to live? You will find the answers in Chapter 8.

Young Mexican girls dance at a festival.

Think, Remember, Write

A. Find the Answer

On your paper, copy each sentence that tells about Mexico's land and people. You should write 7 sentences.

1. The mountains in the west of the United States continue into Mexico.

2. There are mountain chains in the east and in the west of Mexico.

3. Mexico City is in the northern part of the Central Plateau.

4. Most of Mexico's people live in the northern part of the Central Plateau.

5. Mexico City is the largest city in Mexico.

6. The first Mexicans were from Spain.

7. Parents, children, and grandparents often live together in Mexican families.

8. The leader of Mexico's government is the president.

9. Many parts of Mexico have too many mountains and too little rain for farming.

10. Mexico's population is growing slowly.

11. Mexico is a rich country.

12. There are plenty of jobs for people in Mexico.

13. Mexico is a country to the north of the United States.

14. Spanish is the official language of Mexico.

15. Acapulco has cold weather most of the year.

B. Match Up

Finish each question in Group A with an item from Group B. Write the letter of the correct answer on your paper.

<u>Group A</u>

1. _____ is a beach town near the Pacific Ocean.

2. Most Mexicans are _____.

3. The _____ of Mexico is on the east side of the country.

4. Tall _____ make it hard to get to Mexico's natural resources.

5. There is little rain in the _____ part of the Central Plateau.

6. The _____ Plateau is between the mountains in the east and west.

7. People from _____ settled in Mexico.

8. Most of Mexico's people live in the _____ part of the Central Plateau.

9. Mexico's _____ is in Mexico City.

10. _____ is Mexico's most important resource.

11. _____ is the capital of Mexico.

12. The first Mexicans were American _____.

<u>Group B</u>

a. Gulf

b. mestizos

c. Acapulco

d. northern

e. mountains

f. Oil

g. southern

h. Central

i. Spain

j. government

k. Indians

l. Mexico City

C. Locate the Answer

Write the correct answer to each question.

1. What is the official language of Mexico?

   English   French   Spanish

2. Where in Mexico are the rain forests?

   near the Gulf of Mexico   near Acapulco   near Mexico City

3. What does Mexico sell to other countries?

   oil   hats   boots

4. What do farmers grow in the Central Plateau?

   sugar cane and bananas   corn and beans   wheat and oats

5. What is high, flat land?

   mountain   rain forest   plateau

SKILL BUILDER 7: Understanding Hemispheres

Skill Words

hemispheres   Equator   Eastern Hemisphere
Western Hemisphere   Northern Hemisphere
Southern Hemisphere

The earth can be divided into hemispheres, or halves of the earth. There are four hemispheres.

The Equator is a line that is drawn on globes. It is also drawn on world maps. The Equator divides the earth in half at the middle. One half is north of the Equator. This half is called the Northern Hemisphere. The other half is south of the Equator. It is called the Southern Hemisphere.

The earth can also be divided from top to bottom. This forms the Eastern Hemisphere and the Western Hemisphere. North America and South America are in the Western Hemisphere. Europe, Africa, Asia, and Australia are in the Eastern Hemisphere.

Do you live in the United States? You are living in the Western Hemisphere. The United States is north of the Equator. It is also in the Northern Hemisphere.

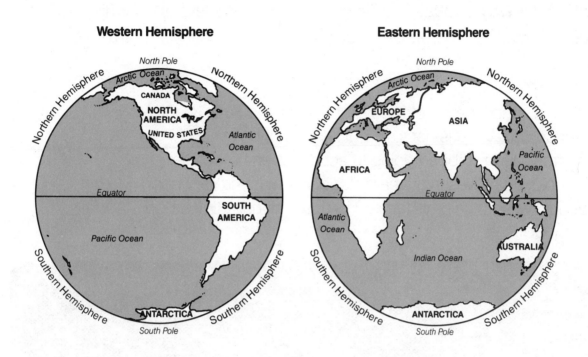

A. Finish the Sentence

Look at the pictures of the four hemispheres on this page. Then write the word that finishes each sentence.

1. The United States is in the ＝＝ Hemisphere.

    Eastern   Western   Southern

2. Europe is in the ＝＝ Hemisphere.

    Eastern   Western   Southern

3. Asia is in the ＝＝ Hemisphere.

    Eastern   Western   Southern

4. Canada is in the ＝＝ Hemisphere.

    Eastern   Northern   Southern

5. Australia is in the ＝＝ Hemisphere.

    Western   Northern   Southern

CHAPTER 8

More About Mexico

NEW WORDS: Juan   village   adults   plantations   fertilizer
crops   market   apartment houses   steel   tourists   mining

It is a school day in Mexico. But 11-year-old Juan is not in school today. He is not sick, but he will not be in school tomorrow. Juan stopped going to school when he was ten years old. Juan lives in a small village. His family is very poor. He must work to help his family. He does not have time to go to school.

A small town in southern Mexico

Most village children in Mexico do not go to school after they are ten years old. Half of Mexico's adults do not know how to read or write. The Mexican government has worked hard to help people learn to read. It has built hundreds of new schools. More and more people are learning to read each year. There are still not enough schools or teachers for all of Mexico's people.

Almost half of Mexico's people work on farms today. Some people work on large farms called plantations. The plantations have new machinery. They use fertilizer to make the soil richer. A lot of Mexico's food is grown on these farms.

In the past most of Mexico's farm land was owned by a few rich Mexicans. The government has tried to help poor people own their own land. The government has bought the land from the rich owners. It has given some of this land to groups of poor people. Groups of farmers work together to grow food. Most of these farmers are still poor. They work the same way farmers worked long ago. They do not have enough money to buy good farm tools or machines. They do not use fertilizer to grow larger crops. Most of these farmers grow just enough food for their families. They have little food to sell to earn money.

This farmer uses animals to pull the plow.

Most Mexican farmers live in villages. A village has a church and a market. People buy and sell goods at the market. Most villages have a school. But some villages have no cars or buses. Some villages do not have electricity.

Every year thousands of poor Mexicans leave their farms and villages. They move to cities. They hope to get better jobs in the cities. The cities are becoming very crowded. There are not enough jobs or houses for all the people.

The government of Mexico is trying to help its people. It has given land to poor farmers. It has built many new roads. The government has built new schools and hospitals. It has built many new apartment houses in the cities.

Thousands of people from the United States and other lands visit Mexico every year. These people are called tourists. They enjoy Mexico's beautiful beaches. They visit Mexico City and other interesting places. Tourists spend a lot of money in Mexico. Mexicans use this money to make their country better.

Mexico is trying to become an industrial country. Many new factories are built each year. More people work in factories. Mexican factories make clothing and paper. They make a strong metal called steel. Steel is made from iron and coal. Many parts for cars are made in Mexican factories. Other things are also made. Mexico sells its factory goods to other

This huge farm uses modern machinery.

countries. Mexico trades with many countries. But it sells more goods to the United States than to any other country.

Mining is important in Mexico. Mining means digging for metals that are deep in the earth. Mexico uses some of its metals for making factory goods. It also sells metals to other countries.

Mexico is still a poor nation. But many Mexicans are living better. Each year more Mexicans get better jobs. They move to better homes. Each year more people learn to read. Mexicans are proud of the way they are working to build a better country.

Think, Remember, Write

A. True or False

Write **T** for each sentence that is true. Write **F** for each sentence that is false.

1. Half of Mexico's adults do not know how to read and write.

2. People who work on small farms grow a lot of food.

3. Poor farmers do not use good tools or fertilizer.

4. Many people are moving out of Mexico's cities.

5. Mexico's government has built schools, hospitals, and apartment houses to help the poor.

6. Not many tourists visit Mexico.

7. Tourists spend a lot of money in Mexico.

8. Mexican factories make clothing, paper, and parts for cars.

9. Mexico buys steel from the United States.

10. Mexico uses some of its metals in its factories and sells metals to other countries.

B. Finish Up

Use the words in dark print to finish each sentence. Write the words you choose on your paper.

tourists   **market**   **steel**   **fertilizer**   **Mining**   **plantations**

1. Very large farms are called _____.

2. Poor farmers do not use good tools or _____.

3. People buy and sell goods at the _____.

4. People called _____ visit Mexico every year.

5. A strong metal that is made from iron and coal is called _____.

6. _____ means digging deep in the earth for metals.

C. Finish the Sentence

Write the word that finishes the sentence.

1. The government of Mexico has given ═══ to poor farmers.

   machinery   land   clothing

2. ═══ of Mexico's adults do not know how to read or write.

   Half   All   One-third

3. Some villages in Mexico do not have ═══ .

   a church   a market   electricity

4. Mexico sells more goods to ═══ than any other country.

   Canada   the United States   Spain

5. Every year thousands of poor Mexicans move to ═══ .

   villages   cities   farms

Skill Words

symbols   map key

Maps can show many things. Sometimes maps use little pictures to show what something on a map means. These pictures are called symbols. A map key tells what the symbols mean.

Look at the map key below.

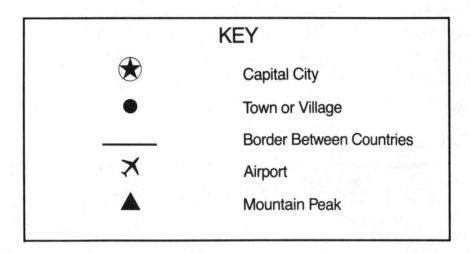

A. Match Up

Match each symbol in Group A with the words that tell what the symbol means in Group B. Write the letter of the correct word on your paper.

Group A

1. ⊛

2. ●

3. ___

4. ✈

5. ▲

Group B

a. Airport

b. Border Between Countries

c. Capital City

d. Mountain Peak

e. Town or Village

CHAPTER 9

Brazil: Giant of South America

NEW WORDS: port   Rio de Janeiro   Portuguese   Europeans
Brazilians   São Paulo   interior   develop   capital   Brasília
imports   exports   sugar cane   cattle

It is a busy day in the port city of Rio de Janeiro. The city
is also called Rio. People are loading ships with goods. Some
ships will carry coffee and sugar. Some will carry nuts and
chocolate. Others will carry factory goods. These ships will
bring goods from Brazil to many countries of the world.

BRAZIL

Brazil is one of Latin America's most important countries. It is one of the world's largest countries. Brazil covers almost half the land of South America. It is nearly as large as the United States.

Brazil has a lot of people. It has more people than all the other countries of South America together. Like Mexico, Brazil's population is growing very fast. Two thirds of the people live in cities. The big cities are very crowded.

Who are the people of Brazil? The American Indians were the first people to live there. Then people from Portugal arrived. Portuguese became the language of Brazil. Brazil is the only Latin American country where people speak Portuguese. The Portuguese brought black slaves from Africa to work in Brazil. People from Japan, and other countries in Europe, have also settled in Brazil.

Rio de Janeiro lies along the Atlantic Ocean.

Today more than half of Brazil's people are of European descent. Brazil has a very small Indian population. There is a large black population. Most Brazilians are Roman Catholics.

Rio de Janeiro is in southern Brazil. It is Brazil's second largest city. The largest city, São Paulo, is also in the south. A large part of Brazil's people live in the southern part of the country. They are within 200 miles *(320 kilometers)* of the Atlantic Ocean. Why do so many people live in the south? Southern Brazil is covered with low plateaus. The weather is comfortable. There is enough rain. There is a lot of good farm land.

Why do fewer people live in northern Brazil? The land of northeastern Brazil gets little rain. It is hot and dry. The soil is not good for farming. Most people there are very poor. The huge Amazon River goes through northern Brazil. Many rivers run into the Amazon. The world's largest rain forest covers a lot of land near the Amazon. The rain forest is hot and very wet. Few people can live there.

The Amazon River

Brazil has a lot of land where few people live. The northern and western areas have few people. The large areas of Brazil that are far from the Atlantic Ocean are called the interior. Much of the interior is covered with forests. Brazil's government wants to develop the interior. It wants people to move to this large part of Brazil.

Many people have already moved to the interior of Brazil. The people moved because their government moved. The city that has a country's government is called the capital. Rio was Brazil's capital city. The government decided to build a new capital city in the interior.

Brasília is the new capital of Brazil. It is in the interior 600 miles *(960 kilometers)* from the ocean. It is far from the other large cities. It was hard to build Brasília. There were no roads or trains to this part of Brazil. New roads were built. Today Brasília is a large, beautiful city. It has many people. But so far few people have moved to other parts of the interior.

Brazil is rich in natural resources. It has many kinds of metals. One fourth of the world's supply of iron is in Brazil. Brazil has lots of trees from its forests and fish from the ocean and rivers. Brazilians make electricity from their water power. Brazil does not have enough oil. It imports, or buys from other countries, most of its oil.

Brasília is the capital of Brazil.

Brazil is an industrial country. It has lots of factories. Cars, steel, clothing, and shoes are a few of the things made in Brazil's factories. Brazil has more factories than any other country in Latin America. Brazil exports, or sells to other countries, its factory goods.

A plastics factory in Brazil

Brazil also exports many farm goods to other countries. Much of the world's coffee, sugar, and chocolate comes from Brazil. It has large coffee and sugar cane plantations. Brazilians raise a lot of cattle. Brazil sells beef from the cattle to other countries. Brazil grows most of the food it needs.

Brazil has farms, factories, and natural resources. These things could make the country rich. But Brazil is a poor country today. A small group of rich people own most of the land and money. Most of Brazil's people are very poor.

There is another reason why Brazil is poor. Brazil's interior has many natural resources. It is hard for people to use the resources of the far-off interior.

In the years ahead, Brazil has two big questions to answer. How can it develop its interior? How can Brazil use its natural resources to become a rich country? The leaders of Brazil are trying to find these answers for their country.

Think, Remember, Write

A. Find the Meaning

Look up each word in a dictionary. Copy one meaning. Then write your own sentence about Brazil for that word.

1. capital

2. develop

3. export

4. import

5. port

B. Write It Right

The words in the sentences below are mixed up. Write each sentence correctly.

1. of South America. Brazil covers the land half almost

2. is population Brazil's fast. very growing

3. of people Two thirds cities. in live Brazil's

4. industrial an country. is Brazil

5. Ocean. miles 200 within Most live Atlantic Brazilians of the

6. rain forest largest is near The world's River. Amazon the

7. supply has iron. large Brazil a of

C. Match Up

Finish each sentence in Group A with an answer from Group B. Write the letter of the correct answer on your paper.

<u>Group A</u>

1. The largest city in Brazil is _____.

2. A large port city is _____.

3. The land of _____ Brazil is very hot and dry.

4. The new capital city in the interior is _____.

5. Large areas of Brazil that are far from the Atlantic are called the _____.

6. Brazil exports coffee, sugar, _____.

7. Brazil is the only Latin American country where people speak _____.

<u>Group B</u>

a. northeastern

b. São Paulo

c. Portuguese

d. interior

e. Rio de Janeiro

f. chocolate and beef

g. Brasília

SKILL BUILDER 9: Reading a Table

Skill Words

table   column   row   heading

A table lists groups of facts. It is easy to compare facts in a table. Facts are grouped down the table in columns. They are grouped across the table in rows. At the top of each column is a heading. It tells what kinds of facts are listed in each column. Another heading is on the left at the beginning of each row. It tells what kinds of facts are grouped in each row. Read the table to learn facts about Brazil, Mexico, and the United States.

Column

		THREE COUNTRIES OF THE WESTERN HEMISPHERE			

Headings →

Country	Population	Largest City	Official Language	Colors of flag
Brazil	128 million	São Paulo	Portuguese	green, yellow, blue
Mexico	76 million	Mexico City	Spanish	red, white, green
United States	232 million	New York City	English	red, white, blue

Row

A. Write the Answer

Use the facts from the table to answer each question.

1. What is the population of Mexico?

2. What are the colors of the Mexican flag?

3. Which country has Portuguese for its official language?

4. What is the population of the United States?

5. What is the largest city in the United States?

6. Which country has the largest population?

7. Which country has the smallest population?

8. What is the official language of Mexico?

9. What is the largest city in Brazil?

CHAPTER 10

Understanding Latin America

NEW WORDS: Mr. Sanchez   Colombia   problem   Argentina   illiteracy   Costa Rica   Haiti   overpopulation   agriculture   one-crop economy   freedom   jail

Mr. Sanchez owns a large coffee plantation in Colombia. Colombia is a South American country that grows a lot of coffee. Mr. Sanchez uses the best machines and fertilizers to grow coffee. He exports his coffee to the United States and Canada. Mr. Sanchez is a very rich man. His children go to fine schools. He has a good life in Colombia.

Hundreds of people work on the Sanchez plantation. The workers are poor. They live in small houses. Their homes do not have electricity. They have small pieces of land that they use to grow food for their families. They do not have good tools. They do not use fertilizer. It is hard for them to grow

Poor families in Latin America

enough food for their families. Most of the children go to school for only a few years.

In Latin America there are hundreds of plantations like the Sanchez plantation. On plantations and in cities, there are big differences between the rich and the poor. These differences are a problem. The rich people have the best food, schools, jobs, and houses. They own most of the land and money. Life is very hard for the millions of poor people.

Some governments are trying to help their poor people live better. In Chapter 8, you learned how Mexico has helped its poor. The country of Argentina is also trying to help its poor. A lot more work is needed to help the poor in Latin America.

Illiteracy is a problem in many parts of Latin America. Illiteracy means people do not know how to read or write. About half the people of Latin America do not know how to read. People who cannot read cannot get good jobs. In some countries like Argentina and Costa Rica, most people can read and write. Other countries have not solved this problem. Haiti is a poor Caribbean country. Most people in Haiti cannot read.

Overpopulation is another problem in many countries. The populations are growing very fast. There is not enough food for all the people. Many people are always hungry. There are not enough jobs, schools, and houses. There are not enough doctors. Cities are becoming very crowded.

You already learned that much of our coffee, sugar, and bananas comes from Latin America. Agriculture is another word for farming. A few countries like Brazil earn money from their factory goods and from agriculture. Some countries earn money from mining and selling metals. But most Latin American countries earn their money from agriculture. Most of their people are poor farmers. Some countries grow only one or two kinds of food. Countries that earn money by growing and selling one kind of food have a one-crop economy.

A one-crop economy can be a big problem. What happens in a year when there is little rain? What happens when the sugar cane crop or coffee crop is poor? The countries with one-crop economies earn little when their crops are poor. It is important for countries to grow and sell many kinds of food. Latin America also needs more factories. People need to earn money by making factory goods.

We learned that the government of Mexico is a democracy. People vote for their government leaders. Mexican laws give the people a lot of freedom. Mexico has a strong government. But there are problems with other Latin American governments today. Many countries are not democracies. People do not choose their leaders. In some countries, army leaders rule the government. There is not much freedom. Sometimes people go to jail for speaking or writing against the government. There is fighting in some countries of Central America today. Groups of people fight to win control of the government. Many people are killed in these fights. Their governments are not strong. The people of Latin America need peace and freedom. They need strong governments.

Houses in La Paz, Bolivia

Latin America is a big land with many natural resources. It has important cities and rivers. It has millions of people. But there are many problems in Latin America. Can the people use their natural resources to solve their problems? In the months ahead, newspaper stories will tell us how Latin Americans are solving their many problems.

Think, Remember, Write

A. True or False

Write **T** for each sentence that is true. Write **F** for each sentence that is false.

1. People who work on plantations have plenty of food.

2. There are few differences between the rich and the poor of Latin America.

3. About half the people of Latin America do not know how to read.

4. Most people in Haiti can read.

5. There is not enough food or schools for all the people of Latin America.

6. All Latin American countries have many factories.

7. Most Latin American countries earn money from agriculture.

8. All the countries of Latin America are democracies.

9. In some countries, people are sent to jail for speaking against the government.

10. In some countries, people fight to win control of the government.

B. Match Up

Finish each sentence in Group A with an answer from Group B. Write the letter of the correct answer on your paper.

<u>Group A</u>

<u>Group B</u>

1. Many poor farmers do not use good machines or _____.

a. crowded

2. The cities of many Latin American countries are very _____.

b. one-crop economy

3. Countries that earn money by growing and selling one kind of food have a _____.

c. illiteracy

d. fertilizer

4. The governments of some countries are not _____.

e. democracies

5. _____ means people do not know how to read or write.

C. Write It Right

The words in the sentences below are mixed up. Write each sentence correctly.

1. populations many are The in fast. countries growing very

2. earn money countries Some selling metals. from mining and

3. earn little crops are poor. when one-crop economies with Countries

4. rule some leaders Army governments. American Latin

Skill Words

grid   squares

A grid is a frame of lines going down and across. The spaces between the lines form squares. We can read the grid like we read a table.

Look at the grid on this page. Like many grids, the squares are named with letters and numbers. Across the top of the grid are letters of the alphabet. Down the side of the grid are numbers. These letters and numbers are the headings of the columns and rows.

To locate a square, just find the place where a column crosses a row. Put your finger on Column B. Move it down to the picture of the mountains. The mountains are in Column B and Row 2. We can say the mountains are in B2.

Put your finger on the mountain picture again. Move your finger to the airport picture. The airport picture is in square C2.

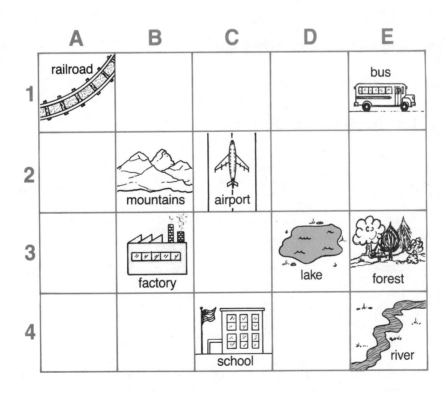

A. Find It

Find the letter and number of the square on the grid for each picture. Write the letter and number on your paper.

1. railroad

2. bus

3. factory

4. forest

5. school

6. river

7. lake

B. Write the Answer

Write the answer for each question.

1. What is a grid?

2. How are the squares on a grid named?

UNIT THREE

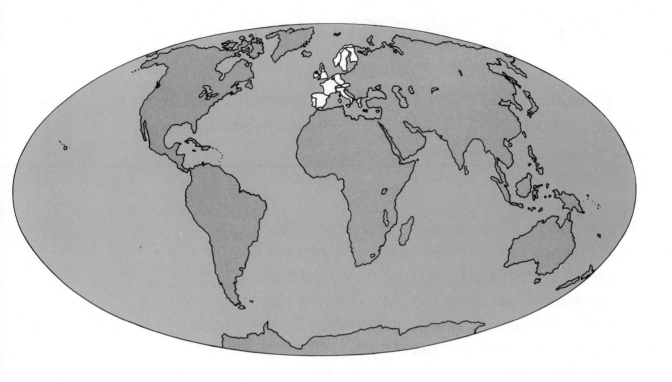

Western Europe

You will read these chapters in Unit 3:

CHAPTER 11

Many Countries on a Small Continent

NEW WORDS: Italy   West Germany   Sweden   world powers
peninsula   North Sea   Mediterranean Sea   coast   climate
Alps   Caucasians   Asians   Jews

An American family wanted to buy a car. They decided
to buy a European car. But there are five countries in Europe
that make cars. From which country did they get their car?

The family's new car came from Italy. Cars are also made
in England and France. They are made in West Germany and
Sweden too. These are just some of the countries that are
part of Western Europe.

Europe is the second smallest continent. Western Europe is

WESTERN EUROPE

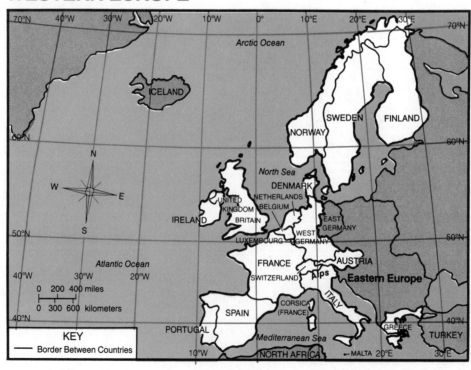

on the western part of the continent of Europe. Western Europe is much smaller than the United States. But it has many more people than the United States. Many languages are spoken in Western Europe.

Western Europe is made up of many countries. Most of the countries there are democracies. In most of these countries, the laws give people a lot of freedom. The countries of Western Europe are small in size. But some of the countries are important world powers. For hundreds of years, the countries of Western Europe have been world leaders.

Western Europe is a large peninsula. A peninsula is a piece of land that has water on three sides. No place in Western Europe is more than 300 miles *(480 kilometers)* away from the sea. The Atlantic and Arctic oceans are to the west and north. The North Sea is also part of Europe. The Mediterranean Sea is to the south. The continent of Asia is to the east.

Windsor Castle in England

Western Europe has a long coast. It has many good ports. For hundreds of years, the seas have helped Europe. People from many countries in Europe used the seas to sail to far-off lands. For hundreds of years, European countries ruled many places in Asia, Africa, and the Americas.

French fishermen unload oysters from their boat.

Europeans used the seas for shipping and trading. Trading ships carry goods from Europe to other lands. They bring goods from other lands back to Europe. Europeans also use the seas for fishing.

The seas have helped Europe in another way. The waters of the Atlantic Ocean that are close to Europe are warm. These waters keep the land of Europe warm. They give Western Europe a good climate. Climate is the kind of weather a place has. Most of Western Europe is not too cold in the winter. It is not too hot in the summer. Most of Western Europe gets enough rain for farming.

There are mountain chains in Western Europe. The most important chain is called the Alps. The mountains of Europe are lower than the Andes Mountains. They are lower than the mountains of the United States and Canada.

There is a lot of good, flat farm land in Europe. Agriculture is important in Western Europe. Many farms are smaller than American farms. Most Europeans add fertilizer to the soil. They use good tools and farm machines. Europeans grow a lot of food on their small farms. Some farm goods are sold to other countries.

Europe's rivers are very important. Rivers are used for transportation. There are port cities along many of the rivers. Ships carry goods from these ports down the rivers to the seas. Then these goods are shipped to other lands.

There are many industrial countries in Western Europe. The countries of Western Europe have a few important natural resources that are used in factories. Water power from Europe's rivers is used to make electricity. Many countries have coal and iron. Coal and iron are used to make steel. Factory goods are sold to many countries.

Who are the people of Europe? Most Europeans are Caucasians, or white people. There are also blacks and Asians in Europe. Most Europeans are Roman Catholics or Protestants. The Jews are another religious group found in Europe.

More than half of Europe's people live in cities. Most Europeans spend many years in school. Almost everyone knows how to read and write. Europe's population is growing slowly. Most people have enough food.

Three of Western Europe's countries are world leaders today. These leading countries are Britain, France, and West Germany. In the next chapters, you will learn why these countries are important.

Think, Remember, Write

A. Find the Answers

On your paper, copy each sentence that tells about Western Europe. You should write 6 sentences.

1. The seas are used for shipping and trading.

2. Ocean water is used to water fields for farming.

3. The seas are used for fishing.

4. The water of the Atlantic Ocean warms the land of Europe.

5. People use ocean water for taking baths.

6. People use the seas to sail to far-off lands.

7. Europe is the second smallest continent.

8. There are no rivers in Western Europe.

9. Western Europe is twice the size of the United States.

10. The Alps are a mountain chain found in Western Europe.

B. Finish Up

Use the words in dark print to finish each sentence. Write the words you choose on your paper.

fertilizers   **climate**   **democracies**
population   **read**   **peninsula**

1. Most of the governments in Western Europe are _____.

2. A _____ is a piece of land that has water on three sides.

3. Most of Western Europe has a good _____ because it is not too cold in the winter or too hot in the summer.

4. European farmers can grow a lot of food because they use _____ and good tools.

5. Europe's _____ is growing slowly.

6. Almost everyone in Europe knows how to _____ and write.

C. Write the Answer

Write a sentence to answer each question.

1. Which 5 countries have car factories?

2. What are the most important mountains in Europe?

3. Why are Western Europe's rivers important? Write 2 sentences.

4. Which 3 countries are world leaders today?

SKILL BUILDER 11: Locating Places on a Grid Map

Skill Words

grid map

Sometimes it is hard to find things on a map. Grids are often drawn on maps to help find places on the map. The map on the next page is a grid map of a town called Green Park. To find a place on the map, look for the square where a column crosses a row. The map shows us that the railroad station is at the corner of Main Street and Lake Street. The grid shows us that the railroad station is in square B4. Where is the high school? It is on Lake Street in square D4.

GREEN PARK

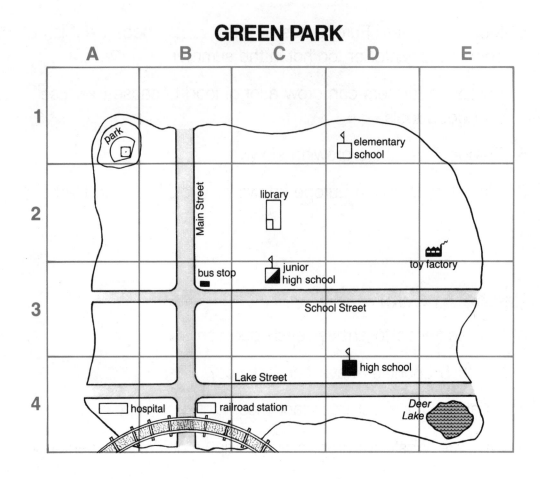

A. Finish the Sentence

Look at the grid map. Then write the word that finishes each sentence.

1. If you put your finger on square C2, you will find the ▬▬.

   library   railroad station   toy factory

2. The park is in square ▬▬.

   A1   B1   E2

3. The junior high school is on ▬▬.

   Main Street   School Street   Lake Street

4. Deer Lake is in square ▬▬.

   D1   C3   E4

5. The bus stop is in square ▬▬.

   D1   E4   B3

CHAPTER 12

Britain: An Island Country

NEW WORDS: British Isles   Britain   English Channel
Scotland   Wales   Northern Ireland   United Kingdom
raw materials   Commonwealth of Nations   Parliament   London

Canada has a queen, but she does not live in Canada. Queen Elizabeth is the queen of many countries. Her home is on the British Isles.

The British Isles are separated from the rest of Europe by the North Sea and the English Channel. Britain is the largest island of the British Isles. England, Scotland, and Wales are on the island of Britain. England is the largest in area. It also has the largest population. England, Scotland, Wales, and Northern Ireland make up the country known as the United Kingdom. The United Kingdom is often called Britain.

BRITAIN

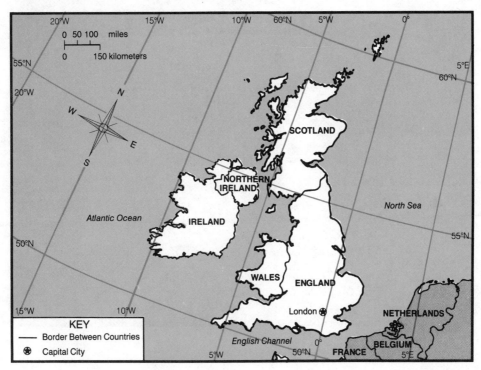

87

The people of Britain are called the British. English is the official language. More than 55 million people live in Britain. Most British people live in cities.

The island of Britain has a long coast. There are many good harbors for shipping. There are many rivers. Britain's rivers are also used for shipping. Most of Britain has a mild climate. The country gets a lot of rain.

Most of Britain's farm land is in southern England. The British are good farmers. But they cannot grow enough food for all the people of Britain. The British must buy half of their food from other countries.

Much of the land of Scotland and Wales is covered with high hills. The soil is poor. Coal mining is important in Wales. Fishing is important in Scotland. Many people in Scotland

Hilly farm land in Britain

work at building ships. People in Scotland and Wales raise sheep. The wool from these sheep is made into cloth.

Britain is not rich in natural resources. It does have some iron ore and natural gas. Some coal is mined in Wales. Britain's most important resource is oil. Britain's oil is under the waters of the North Sea. Britain has all the oil it needs. Britain uses its oil and coal to make electricity.

Britain is also poor in raw materials. Raw materials are things needed to make goods in factories. Wool, wood, and metals are some raw materials. Metals are raw materials that are used to make cars. For many years, Britain has bought raw materials from other countries.

Britain is an important industrial country. It was the first country in the world to become an industrial country. Today British factories make buses, airplanes, and trucks. They also make clothing, dishes, and other things. British goods are sold to many countries.

The seas are important to Britain. It needs the seas for shipping and trading. Britain must buy food and raw materials. Britain earns money by selling factory goods to other countries.

Britain is a member of the Commonwealth of Nations. More than 40 countries belong to the Commonwealth. All of these countries were once ruled by Britain. Now most of them are free countries. But some of them still want Britain's Queen Elizabeth to be their queen. Commonwealth countries trade with each other. They try to help each other.

The people of Britain are proud of their country. Almost everyone can read and write. All children spend many years in school. There is very good transportation in Britain. The British are proud that their small country is a world power.

The British are also proud of their government. It is a strong democracy. British laws are made in a building called Parliament. The British vote for people to make their laws in Parliament. The leader of Parliament is called the prime minister. Britain's government is in England. It is in the city of London. London is Britain's largest city.

The British government meets in Parliament.

Today Britain is a world power with some big problems. Many poor black and Asian people have moved to Britain. These blacks and Asians do not live as well as other British people. The government is trying to find ways to help all its people.

Another problem is that Britain often imports more than it exports. Goods in Britain have become very costly. Britain must find a way to sell more goods to other countries.

The British are proud that their small island country is a world power. They will try hard to solve their problems. They want Britain to be a world leader for many more years.

Think, Remember, Write

A. Finish the Sentence

Write the word that finishes the sentence.

1. The part of Britain with the largest area is ===.

   Wales   England   Scotland

2. Britain's most important natural resource is ===.

   natural gas   iron ore   oil

3. Britain must import a lot of ===.

   coal   wool   raw materials

4. Britain sells === to other countries.

   factory goods   food   natural resources

5. All the countries of the Commonwealth were once ruled by ===.

   Spain   France   Britain

6. The leader of Parliament becomes Britain's ===.

   prime minister   president   queen

7. Britain's government is in the city of === in England.

   Toronto   London   Rio

8. One problem in Britain is that the country is === more goods than it is selling.

   mining   importing   exporting

9. The === is often called Britain.

   English Channel   Commonwealth   United Kingdom

B. Finish Up

Use the words in dark print to finish each sentence. Write the words you choose on your paper.

Wales **Parliament** **oil** **wool** **England**
climate **Elizabeth** **Scotland** **harbors** **Raw**

1. Much of Britain's coal comes from _____.

2. The British get their _____ from the North Sea.

3. The British vote for people to make their laws in _____.

4. The British use _____ to make cloth.

5. _____, Scotland, and Wales are the three countries on the island of Britain.

6. There are good _____ for shipping along Britain's coast.

7. Britain has a mild _____.

8. _____ materials like wool, wood, and metals are needed to make goods in factories.

9. Queen _____ is the queen of Britain and some Commonwealth countries.

10. Fishing and building ships are important in _____.

C. Write It Right

The words in the sentences below are mixed up. Write each sentence correctly.

1. many countries. queen is the of Queen Elizabeth

2. Parliament. building are made in a laws called British

3. of The Parliament. minister is the prime leader

SKILL BUILDER 12: Understanding Latitude

Skill Words

parallels   distance   lines of latitude   degrees

The Equator is an imaginary line that runs around the center of the earth. It runs east and west. There are many more lines that run east and west around the earth. These lines are called parallels. Parallels are always the same distance apart as they go around the earth. Parallels never meet. Parallels on maps and globes are also called lines of latitude. Lines of latitude help us find places on maps and globes. They form part of a grid.

Each line of latitude is named with a number. The number stands for the degrees, or parts of a circle. The Equator is 0 degrees, or 0°. Lines of latitude are also called north or south. There are 90 lines of latitude in the Northern Hemisphere. There are 90 lines of latitude in the Southern Hemisphere. The North Pole is 90° North, or 90°N. Mexico City is also north of the Equator. Its latitude is close to 20°N. The South Pole is 90° South, or 90°S.

LINES OF LATITUDE IN WESTERN EUROPE

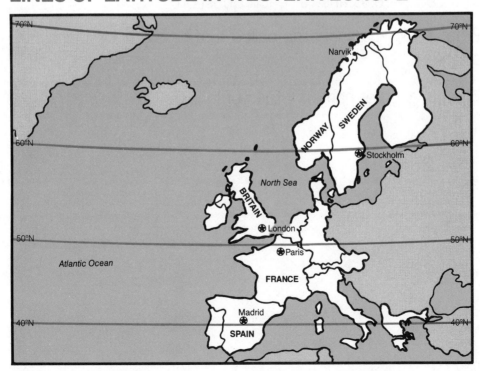

93

A. Match Up

Look at the map on page 93. Finish each sentence in Group A with an answer from Group B. Write the letter of the correct answer on your paper.

<table>
<tr><td>Group A</td><td>Group B</td></tr>
<tr><td>1. Narvik, Norway, is near the .... latitude.</td><td>a. 40°N</td></tr>
<tr><td>2. Stockholm, Sweden, is close to the .... latitude.</td><td>b. 50°N</td></tr>
<tr><td>3. London and Paris are near the .... latitude.</td><td>c. 60°N
d. 70°N</td></tr>
<tr><td>4. Madrid, Spain, is near the .... latitude.</td><td></td></tr>
</table>

B. Write the Answer

Write a sentence to answer each question.

1. What is the imaginary line called that runs around the center of the earth?

2. What is another name for lines of latitude?

CHAPTER 13

France: A World Leader

NEW WORDS: museums   Corsica   Rhône River   canals
Marseille   Pyrenees Mountains   French Riviera   manufacture
perfume   wine   Paris

Two American friends want to visit a country in Western
Europe. One friend wants to be in northern Europe. She
wants to see a big city with museums. The other friend wants
to visit southern Europe. This friend wants to swim at a beach
on the Mediterranean Sea. Can these two friends visit the
same country? The answer is yes if they visit France.

FRANCE

France is one of the powerful countries in Europe. It is the largest country in Western Europe. Northern France is in northern Europe. Southern France is in southern Europe. Corsica is an island in the Mediterranean Sea. It belongs to France. France has a long coast. The Atlantic Ocean is to the west. The Mediterranean Sea is to the south. The English Channel is to the north of France.

France has four important rivers. The most important one is the Rhône River. The rivers of France are used for transportation. Canals join the rivers together. Ships can go from the North Sea down the rivers and canals of France to the city of Marseille. Marseille is an important port on the Mediterranean Sea. France gets water power from the rivers. This water power is used to make electricity.

The city of Marseille lies along the Mediterranean Sea.

More than half of France is covered with flat plains. These plains have very good farm land. France also has tall mountains. There are mountains in the southwest between France and Spain. They are the Pyrenees Mountains. The tall mountains in eastern France are the Alps. Some of these mountains are covered with snow all year long. There are also beautiful beaches in the southeast of France. This part of France is called the French Riviera. It is near the Mediterranean Sea.

Boats and a hotel on the French Riviera

The people of France are very proud of their country. They love their French language. More than 54 million people live in France. France is less crowded than most other countries in Western Europe. Most French people are Roman Catholics. Almost everyone in France knows how to read and write. All children must go to school for ten years.

France is a democracy. The leader of France is the president. The French government meets in their Parliament. The people of France vote for their president. They also vote for people to make their laws in their Parliament.

France has some of the natural resources it needs to be a rich country. It has coal and iron for its factories. France has fish from the seas. It also has forests. France imports oil from other countries. France also imports many raw materials. These raw materials are used in factories.

France is an important industrial country. The French manufacture, or make, steel, clothing, and chemicals. They manufacture cars and airplanes. French goods are sold to many countries. In many countries, people like to drive French cars. Some of the finest perfume and clothing comes from France.

France also has good soil for farming. France grows more food than any other country in Western Europe. The French

France is famous for its vineyards.

use good farm machines and fertilizer. They sell food to many countries. People in many lands eat wheat, fruits, and cheeses from France.

The French also make fine wine. The French grow many kinds of grapes. Many kinds of wine are made from these grapes. The French make more wine than any other country. French wines are sold to many countries.

Most French people live in cities. Paris is the largest city in France. It is also the most important. It is the capital of France. Many factories are in and around Paris.

France is a world power. It has a powerful army. France is a leader in Europe and in the world today.

The Eiffel Tower overlooks Paris.

Think, Remember, Write

A. Locate the Answer

Write the correct answer to each question.

1. Which is the largest country in Western Europe?

   Italy   Sweden   France

2. Where is the French Riviera?

   near the Mediterranean Sea   near the North Sea

   near the Pacific Ocean

3. Which is the largest and most important city in France?

   Paris   London   Marseille

4. What does France import?

   wine   oil   perfume

5. Where do most French people live?

   on farms   in cities   in villages

6. Which country grows the most food in Western Europe?

   France   Britain   Italy

7. What is the official language of France?

   English   French   Latin

8. What is the capital of France?

   Boston   Marseille   Paris

9. What mountains separate France from Spain?

   Pyrenees   Andes   Alps

10. How many years must children attend school in France?

    sixteen   five   ten

B. Write the Answer

Write a sentence to answer each question.

1. Which island in the Mediterranean belongs to France?

2. For what are the rivers of France used? Write 2 sentences.

3. What kind of land covers more than half of France?

4. What are some of France's natural resources?

5. What do the French manufacture? Write 2 sentences.

C. Finish Up

Use the words in dark print to finish each sentence. Write the words you choose on your paper.

Spain   **Parliament**   **Canals**
     wine   **French Riviera**

1. _____ join the rivers of France together.

2. France has mountains in the southwest that separate France from _____.

3. There are beautiful beaches on the _____.

4. France is a democracy with a president and _____.

5. The French make fine _____ from many kinds of grapes.

SKILL BUILDER 13: Understanding Longitude

Skill Words

meridians   lines of longitude   Greenwich, England
Prime Meridian   Hamburg, West Germany

You learned that lines of latitude run east and west around the earth.

There are also lines that run north and south around the earth. North and south lines are called meridians. They are also called lines of longitude.

Lines of longitude are farthest apart at the Equator. They are closer to each other as they move toward the North and South poles. Lines of longitude meet at the poles.

The most important line of longitude runs through Greenwich, England. It is called the Prime Meridian. Lines of longitude are named with their number of degrees, just like lines of latitude. The Prime Meridian is 0 degrees, or 0°. Lines of longitude are also called east or west. There are 180 lines of longitude that are east of the Prime Meridian. There are 180 lines of longitude to the west. Hamburg is a city in West Germany. Hamburg is east of the Prime Meridian. Its longitude is 10° East, or 10°E. The city of Rio de Janeiro in Brazil is west of Greenwich. Rio's longitude is 40° West, or 40°W.

LINES OF LONGITUDE IN WESTERN EUROPE

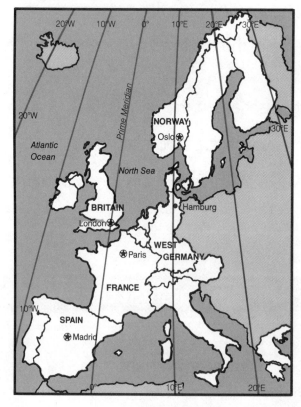

A. Locate the Answer

Look at the map of Western Europe. Then read the sentences below. Write the correct answer to each question.

1. What is the longitude of London?

   120°W   0°   40°E

2. What is the longitude of Hamburg, West Germany?

   10°E   180°E   150°W

3. Between what lines of longitude is Madrid, Spain?

   100°-110°W   140°-150°E   10°W-0°

4. What line of longitude is close to Oslo, Norway?

   10°E   60°E   140°W

5. What line of longitude is near Paris, France?

   170°W   90°E   0°

B. Mixed-up Words

The letters in the words below have been mixed up. Rewrite the words correctly. A list of the correct words is on the right.

1. imrPe Mdeiiran   Equator

2. orhtN Ploe   South Pole

3. utaroEq   North Pole

4. thouS ePlo   Prime Meridian

CHAPTER 14

West Germany: An Industrial Leader

NEW WORDS: modern   ruins   World War II   Soviet Union
Berlin   rebuilt   chancellor   Bonn

Which country has the most factories in Western
Europe? Which country exports more goods than any other
country in Western Europe? Which country has the largest
population in Western Europe? The answer to all three
questions is West Germany.

West Germany is a crowded country. More than 61 million
people live there. They speak the German language. Almost

WEST GERMANY

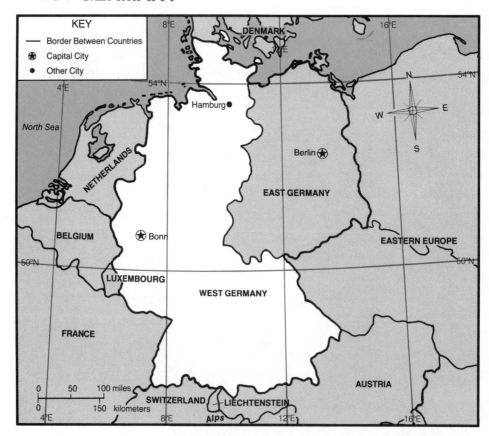

everyone knows how to read and write. All children must spend ten years in school.

West Germany looks very different today than it did in the year 1945. Today West Germany is a country with modern cities and farms. In 1945 much of Germany was in ruins. It had been damaged in World War II.

At the end of World War II, Germany was divided into two countries. One country was East Germany. The Soviet Union controlled this country. The other part became West Germany. Most of the time, people in the two Germanys are not allowed to visit each other.

This wall separates West Berlin from East Berlin.

The German city of Berlin was also divided after the war. Berlin is a big city in East Germany. East Berlin is now the capital of East Germany. West Berlin is a free city. It does not belong to East or West Germany. There is travel and trade between West Germany and West Berlin.

West Germany was rebuilt after World War II. Cities, farms, and railroads were rebuilt. Old factories were rebuilt. Many new factories were started. Today West Germany is a rich country. It is a great industrial country. There are factories in almost every part of West Germany. The factories are large and modern.

West German factories make many goods. They make steel, cars, ships, and planes. They make machines and chemicals. West Germany sells its goods to many countries. The United States is the only country in the world that sells more goods to other countries than West Germany.

West Germany is a leading maker of cars.

West Germany is not rich in natural resources. Germans import most of the resources they need. They import all of their oil. But they do have lots of coal. They use this coal to make steel and electricity.

There are more than one million farms in West Germany. The Germans are good farmers. But they cannot grow all the food that they need. They must buy some of their food from other countries in Europe.

West Germany has sea ports, flat farm land, and tall mountains. Northern Germany is near the North Sea. The land in the north is flat. Southern Germany has hills and mountains. The tall Alps cover part of southern Germany.

After World War II, West Germany became a democracy. The government of West Germany is its Parliament. The leader of the government is called the chancellor. The capital is in the city of Bonn.

There is fine transportation in West Germany. There are roads, airports, and railroads. Rivers and canals are also used for transportation. The city of Hamburg is a port on the North Sea. River ships carry factory goods to Hamburg. From Hamburg, these goods are shipped to many countries.

There are problems in West Germany today. Most Germans are unhappy that their country was divided. It is hard for families in the two Germanys to visit each other.

There are other problems too. For a few years, there were not enough Germans to work at all the factory jobs. Many people from poorer countries came to work in West Germany. They came from other parts of Europe and North Africa. It is a big job to help these workers learn how to live in West Germany.

In 1983 there was a new problem. There were not enough jobs for all the people. Many people were not able to work and earn money. The Germans are working on these problems. In the years ahead, West Germany will be an important country in Europe. It will also be one of the world's great industrial countries.

Think, Remember, Write

A. Match Up

Finish each sentence in Group A with an answer from Group B. Write the letter of the correct answer on your paper.

<table>
<tr><td>Group A</td><td>Group B</td></tr>
</table>

Group A

1. _____ is a free city that does not belong to East or West Germany.

2. After World War II, West Germany became a _____.

3. The capital of West Germany is _____.

4. The leader of West Germany's government is called the _____.

5. The city of _____ is a port near the North Sea.

Group B

a. chancellor

b. Hamburg

c. democracy

d. Bonn

e. West Berlin

B. Finish Up

Use the words in dark print to finish each sentence. Write the words you choose on your paper.

coal   **German**   **rebuilt**   **modern**

1. The people of Germany speak the _____ language.

2. After World War II, much of Germany had to be _____.

3. Today West Germany has many _____ factories.

4. Most electricity in West Germany is made by using _____.

C. True or False

Write **T** for each sentence that is true. Write **F** for each sentence that is false.

1. West Germany has the largest population in Western Europe.

2. Every part of West Germany has flat farm land.

3. German factories make steel, cars, ships, planes, and chemicals.

4. West Germany exports more factory goods than any other country in Western Europe.

5. West Germany is rich in oil and other natural resources.

6. It is easy for people in East and West Germany to visit each other.

7. West Germans grow all the food they need.

8. In 1983 there were not enough jobs for all the people in West Germany.

SKILL BUILDER 14: Using Latitude and Longitude

Skill Words
locations

You learned that lines of latitude are east and west lines around the earth. Lines of longitude are north and south lines. Lines of latitude and longitude form grids on maps and globes. These grids make it easy to find locations, or where places are, on maps and globes.

The latitude of a place is written first. Then the longitude is written next to it. The latitude of Rio de Janeiro, Brazil, is 23°S. Its longitude is 40°W. The latitude and longitude of Rio are 23°S, 40°W. What is the location of Hamburg, West Germany? Its latitude is 53°N. Its longitude is 10°E. The latitude and longitude of Hamburg are 53°N, 10°E.

The latitude and longitude of a place also tells in which hemisphere the place is. We know that Rio's location is 23°S, 40°W. This tells us that Rio is in the Southern and Western hemispheres. Hamburg's location is 53°N, 10°E. Hamburg is in the Northern and Eastern hemispheres.

LINES OF LATITUDE AND LONGITUDE IN WESTERN EUROPE

A. Which Latitude or Longitude?

Look at the map of Western Europe. Use the latitudes and longitudes in dark print to finish each sentence. Write the words you choose on your paper.

0°   48°N   60°N

1. The latitude and longitude of Paris, France, are ═══ , 2°E.

2. The location of London, England, is 51°N, ═══ .

3. The location of Oslo, Norway, is ═══ , 10°E.

B. Which Hemisphere?

Finish each sentence with the words **Northern, Southern, Eastern, Western.** Write the correct word on your paper.

1. The latitude and longitude of Montreal are 45°N, 74°W. The city is in the _____ and Western hemispheres.

2. New York City's location is 40°N, 73°W. The city is in the Northern and _____ hemispheres.

3. São Paulo's location is 23°S, 46°W. The city is in the _____ and Western hemispheres.

4. Hamburg's location is 53°N, 10°E. The city is in the Northern and _____ hemispheres.

5. Berlin's location is 52°N, 13°E. The city is in the _____ and Eastern hemispheres.

6. The longitude and latitude of Wellington, New Zealand are 41°S, 174°E. This city is in the _____ and Eastern hemispheres.

CHAPTER 15

Understanding Western Europe

NEW WORDS: Swedish   peace   Common Market   unite   tariffs   tax   NATO

Let's visit two farms in Western Europe. The first farm is in Sweden. Only a small part of Sweden's land is good for farming. But Swedish farmers use good tools and fertilizers. They are able to grow a lot of food. The second farm is in Portugal. These farmers are poor. They work the same way farmers worked a hundred years ago. They do not have modern tools or machines. This farm does not grow as much food as the farm in Sweden.

The headquarters of the Common Market is in Belgium.

There are many differences between the countries of Western Europe. Some countries like Sweden are rich. Other countries like Portugal are poorer. The people speak different languages. Each country has its own laws and leaders. Each country in Western Europe has its own money. Every country has its own flag.

There are religious differences in Western Europe too. Most people in southern Europe are Roman Catholics. Most people in northern Europe belong to Protestant churches. There are Jews in many parts of Western Europe. There are also people who belong to other religions.

There is peace in Western Europe today. But for hundreds of years, there were wars between the countries of Europe. Sometimes countries fought to rule other lands. More than 200 years ago, England and France fought to rule America. Most countries in Europe fought in World War II. Much of Europe was destroyed. People of different religious groups have fought in Western Europe too. Today there is some fighting in Northern Ireland.

The countries of Western Europe want to have peace for many years. Many countries are trying to work together and help each other. Some people hope that one day all the countries of Europe will unite to become one country. Some people hope that one day there will be a United States of Europe.

The countries of Western Europe are already working together. In 1957 a group of countries formed the European Economic Community. It is also called the Common Market. Today there are ten countries in the Common Market. More countries may join.

The Common Market helps its members. Trade is very important to all the countries of Western Europe. In the past, countries had to pay tariffs on goods they bought from other countries. A tariff is a tax. It is extra money people must pay for goods that come from other countries. Tariffs make goods more costly. Tariffs make it harder for people to buy goods from other lands. The Common Market helped its members by removing tariffs. Common Market members do not pay tariffs on goods they buy from each other. They do not pay tariffs on goods that they sell to each other. All Common Market countries now have more trade with each other.

The Common Market has made it easier for people to work in different countries. It is easy for someone in Italy to get a job in Germany. A person in France can start a business in England.

The countries of Western Europe have also joined together to protect each other if there should be a war. Most of the countries belong to NATO. These letters stand for the North Atlantic Treaty Organization. The United States and Canada also belong to NATO.

The countries of Western Europe are also joined by good transportation. Roads connect all parts of Europe. Railroads connect many countries. Europe has many airports. People fly from one city in Europe to another.

Fast trains connect the big cities of Europe.

Europeans enjoy visiting the different countries of Western Europe. People from many countries like to visit the French Riviera. Other people like to ski on the Alps.

Many people vacation on the French Riviera.

The people of Western Europe are proud of their countries. They are proud of the languages they speak. But they are also proud to be Europeans. Can the many countries of Western Europe form one country? This has not yet happened. But perhaps one day there will be a country called the United States of Europe.

Think, Remember, Write

A. Write It Right

The words in the sentences below are mixed up. Write each sentence correctly.

1. Europe. in many of Jews There Western are parts

2. were wars there hundreds For of years of Europe. countries the between

3. hope one there a States people that of Europe. United Some day will be

4. harder people for goods lands. other it make Tariffs to buy from

5. visiting Europe. Western Europeans countries enjoy of the different

B. Find the Answer

On your paper, copy the sentences that tell about the countries of Western Europe. You should write 4 sentences.

1. Some countries like Sweden are rich, but others like Portugal are poor.

2. All countries in Western Europe use the same money.

3. Many languages are spoken in Western Europe.

4. Most people in northern Europe are Protestants.

5. The chancellor of West Germany rules all of Western Europe.

6. The Common Market has made it harder for people to work in different countries.

7. All the countries of NATO are in Western Europe.

8. People from many countries visit the French Riviera.

C. Write the Answer

Write a sentence to answer each question.

1. How many countries are in the Common Market?

2. What is a tariff?

3. How has the Common Market helped its members? Write 2 sentences.

4. What have NATO members promised to do?

Skill Words

graphs   compare   bar graphs

   Graphs are special drawings. They show facts by using lines, shapes, colors, or symbols. Graphs help us compare facts. The drawing on this page is called a bar graph. It shows the facts with bars of different lengths. This bar graph shows populations. By looking at the length of the bars, you can see the population of each country. You can also compare the populations of the three countries.

POPULATIONS OF BRITAIN, FRANCE, AND WEST GERMANY

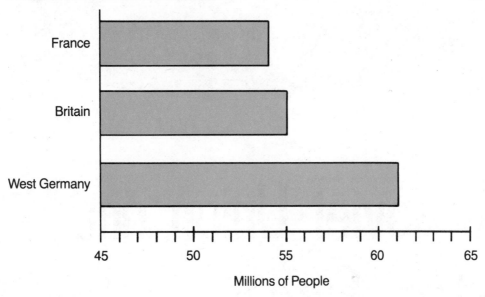

Millions of People

A. Write the Answer

Look at the bar graph. Then write the answer to each question.

1. What is the population of France?

2. What is the population of Britain?

3. What is the population of West Germany?

4. Which country has the largest population?

5. Which country has the smallest population?

UNIT FOUR

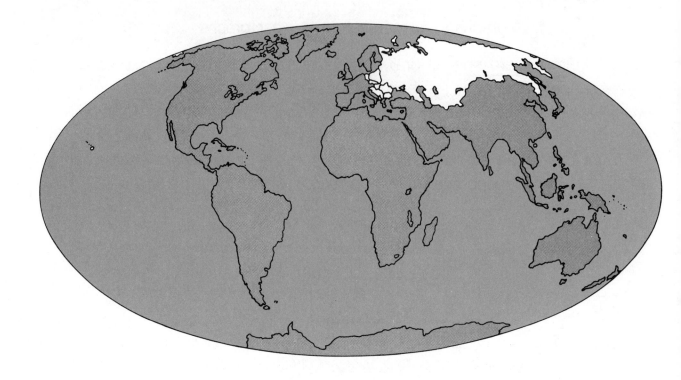

The Soviet Union and Eastern Europe

You will read these chapters in Unit 4:

CHAPTER 16

Eastern Europe

NEW WORDS: Communists   dominated   Yugoslavia   Albania
consumer goods   state farms   collectives   Communist party
practice their religion

The big cities of Eastern Europe are a lot like big cities in
Western Europe. They have lots of people, many stores, and
many buses. But there are not as many cars on the streets of
Eastern Europe. In Western Europe, many people have their
own cars. In Eastern Europe, fewer people own cars. Eastern
Europe is ruled by people called Communists.

The city of Prague, Czechoslovakia

Eastern Europe is the land on the eastern part of the
continent of Europe. The Soviet Union is to the east of Eastern
Europe. There are eight countries in Eastern Europe. Six of
these countries are dominated by the Soviet Union.
Yugoslavia and Albania are two countries that are not
controlled by the Soviet Union.

Most of Eastern Europe is farther from the Atlantic Ocean than Western Europe. This makes most of Eastern Europe colder than Western Europe. There is not as much rain for farming. Not as much food is grown.

There are flat plains and mountains in Eastern Europe. The northern part of Eastern Europe is covered with plains. A lot of good farm land is on these plains. Many places in the southern part of Eastern Europe are covered with mountains.

Eastern Europe does not have many natural resources. The countries buy some of their resources from the Soviet Union. But Eastern Europe does have coal. It also has water power from its rivers.

All the countries of Eastern Europe are ruled by Communist governments. In a Communist country, most land is owned by the government. The government owns all factories, stores, and businesses. The government decides what should be made in factories. The government decides how much things should cost. It decides how much workers should be paid.

Factories in Communist lands make steel. They also make weapons and machines. Factories in Communist countries do

A machinery factory in East Germany

120

not make many consumer goods. Consumer goods are things that are used directly by people. Some consumer goods are clothing, cars, washing machines, and radios. Factories in Communist lands do not make many cars, washing machines, or radios. It is hard for people to own these things.

Farming is different in most Communist lands too. In most of these countries, people are not allowed to have their own farms. Many farms are owned by the government. These farms are called state farms. State farms are very large. The government pays for the farm machines. The government also pays the workers on state farms.

Other Communist farms are called collectives. A collective is a large farm. Many people work on a collective. These people share the money that the farm makes. They use some of the money the farm makes to buy farm machines and fertilizer.

Workers plant seeds on this farm in Hungary.

The countries of Eastern Europe are not democracies. Every country is ruled by a Communist party. A Communist party is a group of people who want a Communist government. There is little freedom in Communist Europe. People are not allowed to speak against their government. All books and newspapers must agree with what the government does. Communist leaders are against religion. It is hard for people to practice their religion in Communist lands.

The Soviet Union dominates most of the countries of Eastern Europe. The Soviet Union is the world's largest country. It is one of the most powerful countries in the world. What is it like to live in this huge Communist land? You will find the answers in Chapters 17 and 18.

Think, Remember, Write

A. Finish Up

Use the words in dark print to finish each sentence. Write the words you choose on your paper.

southern   **collective**   **northern**   **coal**
Consumer goods   **Atlantic Ocean**   **State farms**

1. Eastern Europe is colder than Western Europe because it is farther from the _____.

2. There are plains in the _____ part of Eastern Europe.

3. Many places in the _____ part of Eastern Europe are covered with mountains.

4. The important natural resources of Eastern Europe are _____ and water power.

5. People who work on a _____ share the money that the farm makes.

6. _____ are owned by the government, and people are paid to work on them.

7. _____ are things like clothing and radios that are used directly by people.

B. True or False

Write **T** for each sentence that is true. Write **F** for each sentence that is false.

1. Communist governments own all factories, stores, and businesses.

2. Communist governments decide how much workers should be paid.

3. Communist governments decide what should be made in factories.

4. There is a lot of freedom in Communist countries.

5. Every Communist country is ruled by a Communist party.

6. Most farmers have their own farms in Communist countries.

7. Communist leaders want people to practice their religion.

C. Write It Right

The words in the sentences below are mixed up. Write each sentence correctly.

1. ruled Eastern people by Communists. called is Europe

2. countries by dominated Six Union. Eastern Soviet in Europe the are

3. machines make countries Factories Communist in and weapons.

4. hard practice lands. in for It Communist religion their to people is

SKILL BUILDER 16: Understanding Borders on Political Maps

Skill Words

borders   political map   national border

Some lines are drawn on maps and globes to show borders. These lines show how land is divided. Some borders show how land is divided between countries. Borders between countries are called national borders. Other borders show how land is divided between states and cities.

Borders are an important part of political maps. Political maps show how areas of the earth are divided into countries. Some political maps show only a small part of a country. Other maps show many countries.

Look at the political map of Eastern Europe. The dark lines show the borders between the countries. Trace the borders with a pen or pencil.

A. Locate the Answer

Write the correct answer to each question.

1. Which lines show how land is divided into countries?

   parallels   borders   meridians

2. What is a national border?

   the border of a city   the border of a country

   the border of a state

3. Areas of the earth are divided into what on political maps?

   climate areas   mountain ranges   countries

4. What symbol is used on the map to show a national border?

   a black line   little circles   little houses

EASTERN EUROPE

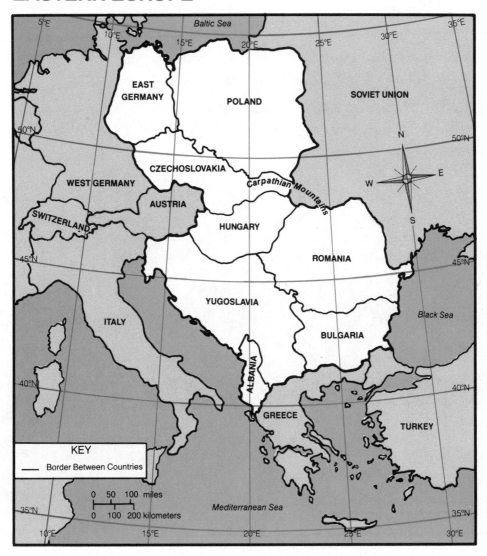

CHAPTER 17

The Soviet Union

NEW WORDS: Moscow   Lenin's Tomb   hero   Ural Mountains
Union of Soviet Socialist Republics   Soviets   Siberia   tundra
Black Sea   Odessa   Volga River   Caspian Sea   republic
Russia

Every day of the year people stand in line in Moscow.
Moscow is the capital of the Soviet Union. People there wait
to visit Lenin's Tomb. Lenin was the leader who helped the
Soviet Union become a Communist country. Today he is a
great hero to the Soviet people.

Soldiers march past a huge poster of Lenin.

The Union of Soviet Socialist Republics is the official name
of the Soviet Union. The Soviet Union is the world's largest
country. This large country is on two continents. The western
part of the Soviet Union is in Europe. The eastern part is in

Asia. The Ural Mountains separate the European part from the Asian part. There are also mountains in the south.

The Soviet Union has 270 million people. Only two countries in the world have more people than the Soviet Union. Most Soviets live in the European part of the country. Most large cities are in this part of the country.

A large part of the Soviet Union is very cold. Most places are far north of the Equator. They are also far from the warm waters of the Atlantic Ocean. Most places have long, cold winters. Almost half of the land is always frozen. Soviet land in northern Asia is called Siberia. One half of all Soviet land is in Siberia.

There are many kinds of land in the Soviet Union. Much of the country is covered with flat plains. The northern plains have cold, icy land. This icy land is called tundra. It is too cold there for trees to grow. South of the tundra are thick forests. There are grassy plains with good farm land south of the forests. There are dry deserts in the south of the country. The Soviet Union also has warm beaches near the Black Sea.

The Soviet Union has a long coast. But there are few ports that are good for shipping. The cold Arctic Ocean is to the north of the Soviet Union. The Pacific Ocean is to the east. Most of the water near the coast is filled with ice for many months each year. The ice makes it hard for ships to sail from the ports. The Soviet Union does have an important port on the Black Sea. It is called Odessa. From Odessa, ships sail south. They can sail into the Mediterranean Sea.

The Soviet Union is very rich in natural resources. The Soviet Union has almost everything it needs for its factories. Many resources are found in cold Siberia. There are large amounts of coal and natural gas. The Soviet Union has all the oil it needs. It has gold, iron, and other metals. There is water power from the rivers and fish from the lakes.

Transportation is important in this huge country. But it is easier to travel in the European part of the country. This part of the Soviet Union has many roads and railroads. Rivers in the west are used for transportation too. The Volga River is the longest river in Europe. It starts near Moscow and flows south to the Caspian Sea.

There is less transportation in the Asian part of the Soviet Union. It is hard to build roads and railroads on the frozen land. There is only one railroad that runs across Siberia. The Soviets often use airplanes to get across their huge country.

This train is on the Trans-Siberian Railroad.

The Soviet Union is made up of 15 states. These states are called republics. Different languages are spoken in the different republics. Most Soviet land is in the republic called Russia. It is the largest republic. More than half of all Soviet people are Russians. They speak the Russian language. Russian is the official language of the Soviet Union. Children in every republic must study the Russian language in school. Russia is the most important part of the Soviet Union. Sometimes the whole country is called Russia.

The Soviet Union was the first country in the world to have a Communist government. The Communists control every part of Soviet life. What is it like to live in this huge Communist land? You will find the answers in the next chapter.

Think, Remember, Write

A. Find the Answer

On your paper, copy the sentences that tell about the Soviet Union. You should write 4 sentences.

1. Soviet land in northern Asia is called Siberia.

2. All the land in the Soviet Union is always frozen.

3. The Soviet Union is very rich in natural resources.

4. The Soviet Union must buy all of its oil from other countries.

5. The Soviet Union has many warm water ports.

6. Tall mountains separate the European part of the Soviet Union from the Asian part.

7. Russia is the largest republic in the Soviet Union.

B. Write It Right

The words in the sentences below are mixed up. Write each sentence correctly.

1. is covered Soviet Union Most of the plains. flat with

2. land Siberia. One all half of in Soviet is

3. land without trees icy is Cold, tundra. called

4. the Arctic near of the year. water coast The ice with is months for many filled

C. Write the Answer

Write a sentence to answer each question.

1. What is the capital of the Soviet Union?

2. Which mountains separate the European part of the Soviet Union from the Asian part?

3. What is an important port city on the Black Sea?

4. How many republics are in the Soviet Union?

5. What is the official name of the Soviet Union?

SKILL BUILDER 17: Reading Symbols on a Political Map

Skill Words

Finland   China   Trans-Siberian Railroad

A map key is an important part of a political map. The map key shows what the symbols on the map mean. Look at the political map of the Soviet Union. There are symbols on the map. The map key helps us understand these symbols.

A. Finish the Sentence

Write the word that finishes the sentence.

1. The Soviet border with China is to the === of the Soviet Union.

   north   west   south

2. The Soviet border with Finland is to the === of the Soviet Union.

   northwest   southwest   northeast

3. The symbol for a capital city is ═══.

   a star   a circle   a triangle

4. Most of the Trans-Siberian Railroad is in the ═══ of the Soviet Union.

   north   south   west

5. Novosibirsk is a ═══ in Siberia.

   city   mountain   capital city

THE SOVIET UNION

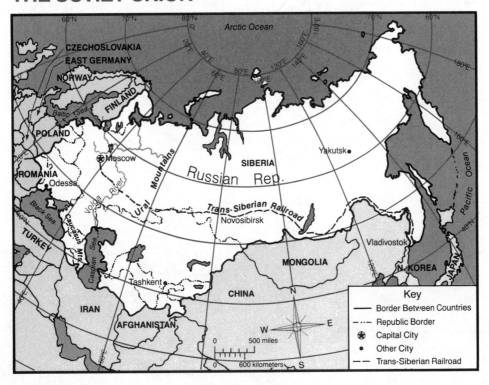

CHAPTER 18

More About the Soviet Union

NEW WORDS: Yuri   Israel   punished   permission   churches
synagogues   university   members

Yuri is a man who lives in a jail in Siberia. A few years
ago he lived in Moscow. Yuri is a Soviet Jew. He was not
happy in the Soviet Union. He asked his government if he
could move to a country called Israel. Soviet laws do not
allow people to move to other countries. The government
punished Yuri because he wanted to leave.

Life is very hard for the Jews of the Soviet Union. There
are more than two million Jews there. It is harder for them to
get good jobs or go to good schools than for other Soviet
people. Many Soviet Jews are now in jail because they tried
to practice their religion. Others are in jail because they asked
to leave the Soviet Union.

Moscow is the capital of the Soviet Union.

There is little freedom for most people in the Soviet Union. People cannot speak or write against their country. Few people can visit other countries. People are not allowed to move to other countries. They need permission to move to a different city. It is hard for people to practice their religion. Many churches and synagogues have been closed.

The Communist government controls life in the Soviet Union. People cannot own their own farms. Many people work on state farms. Other people work on collectives. The Soviet Union has more farm land than any other country. But it does not grow enough food for its people. The Soviet Union imports food from other countries. It buys wheat and corn from the United States.

People who work on collectives are allowed to own very small pieces of farm land. They can work on their land only during their free time. These small pieces of land are only a very small part of the farm land in the country. But one third of all Soviet food is grown there.

All Soviet factories are controlled by the government. These factories make steel and machines. They make airplanes, trucks, and many kinds of weapons. They do not make many consumer goods.

The Communists did not always rule the Soviet Union. They became the leaders in 1917. Before 1917 most Soviets were very poor. Most people did not know how to read. Most people did not have enough food. The Communists helped the country become an industrial country. Today most people have enough food. The government pays doctors to care for people.

School is very important to the people of the Soviet Union. Everyone knows how to read and write. Soviet children go to school six days a week. They go to school during most of the summer. People must study in a university to get a good job in the Soviet Union.

The Soviet Union is ruled by its Communist party. The leader of the party leads the country. This leader has a lot of power. Members of the Communist party get the best jobs and houses. They are allowed to shop in special stores. These stores have more consumer goods. It is easier for party members to own cars. Their children go to better schools. Only a small part of the population is allowed to join the party.

The Communists in the Soviet Union want more countries to have Communist governments. Sometimes they send soldiers and weapons to people in other countries. They want people to use the weapons to fight for new Communist governments. The United States and other free countries do not like what the Soviet Communists are trying to do. They want the countries of the world to be free.

A large department store in Moscow

Think, Remember, Write

A. Finish Up

Use the words in dark print to finish each sentence. Write the words you choose on your paper.

republic   Communist   farm   six
1917   university   party   third
consumer   city   Jews   churches

1. Most _____ and synagogues in the Soviet Union have been closed.

2. The Soviet Communists want other countries to have _____ governments.

3. Russia is the largest _____ in the Soviet Union.

4. One _____ of the food in the Soviet Union is grown on very small pieces of land.

5. Soviet factories make more steel and weapons than _____ goods.

6. People who go to a _____ get better jobs.

7. Only a small part of the Soviet people can belong to the Communist _____.

8. Life is very hard for the _____ of the Soviet Union.

9. Soviet children go to school _____ days a week.

10. The Soviet Union has more _____ land than any other country.

11. Soviet people must get permission to move to a different _____.

12. The Soviet Union has been a Communist country since _____.

B. True or False

Write **T** for each sentence that is true. Write **F** for each sentence that is false.

1. Soviet people can move anywhere they want to move.

2. The Soviets grow more food than they need.

3. The Communists have helped the Soviet Union become an industrial country.

4. Members of the Communist party get better jobs and houses.

5. Sometimes the Soviet Communists send soldiers and weapons to other countries.

6. The United States and other free countries do not like the Soviet Union helping to set up other Communist governments.

C. Match Up

Finish each sentence in Group A with an answer from Group B. Write the letter of the correct answer on your paper.

Group A

1. People in the Soviet Union are not allowed to _____.

2. All Soviet factories are _____.

3. The Soviets import wheat from _____.

4. Many Soviet Jews are in jail because they _____.

Group B

a. have their own farms

b. the United States

c. asked to leave the Soviet Union

d. controlled by the government

136

SKILL BUILDER 18: Understanding a Distance Scale on a Town Map

Skill Words

distance scale   inch   mile

A distance scale is an important part of a map. We want to know the distance when we try to learn how far apart two places are. A distance scale helps us find the distance between places on a map. The map on this page shows the town of Deer Water. The distance scale tells us that one inch on this map is the same as one mile in the real town. There are two inches between the hospital and the shoe factory on this map. In the real town, these places would be two miles apart.

DEER WATER

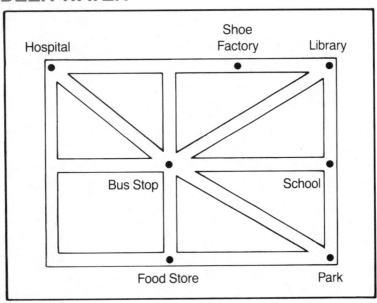

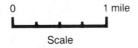

A. Finish the Sentence

Use your ruler to measure the distances between places on the map of Deer Water. Then write the word that finishes the sentence.

1. The library and the school are ═══ apart.

   1 inch   2 inches   3 inches

2. The distance between the library and the school is ═══.

   1 mile   2 miles   3 miles

3. The library and the hospital are ═══ apart.

   1 inch   2 inches   3 inches

4. The distance between the library and the hospital is ═══.

   1 mile   2 miles   3 miles

5. The distance between the bus stop and the park is ═══.

   1 mile   2 miles   3 miles

CHAPTER 19

Poland: A Soviet Neighbor

NEW WORDS: Poland   Baltic Sea   Polish   Czechoslovakia
Vistula River   Poles   Warsaw   privately owned   trade unions
Solidarity

It is Sunday morning in Poland. The churches are filled
with people. Poland is different from other countries in Eastern
Europe. The Communists have not been able to stop people
from practicing their religion. Most people in Poland are
Roman Catholics. People care a lot about religion in
Communist Poland.

It is a cold, wet day in Warsaw.

Poland is the largest country in Eastern Europe. Most of
Poland is covered with flat plains. The Baltic Sea is to the
north. There are ports and beaches on the Baltic Sea. Tall
mountains are in the south. These mountains are between
Poland and Czechoslovakia. East Germany is to the west of
Poland. The Soviet Union is to the east.

The Vistula River is the most important river in Poland. It runs from the mountains in the south to the Baltic Sea. This river is used for transportation.

There are 37 million people in Poland today. The people of Poland are called Poles. They speak the Polish language. Warsaw is Poland's largest city. It is also the capital. Poland's Communist leaders work there. Most of Warsaw was destroyed during World War II. After the war, the Poles rebuilt their city.

Catholics gather for a church service in Poland.

Poland is an industrial country. But all factories and stores are owned by the government. The Communist leaders decide what each factory will make. They decide how much things will cost. Like other Communist countries, there are not many consumer goods.

The government decides what kind of home a person or family will have. It decides how many rooms a family needs. A large family will be given a large apartment. A family with only one or two children will have a small apartment.

Farming is important in Poland. There are some collectives and state farms. But most farms are privately owned. The farms are small. Poland and Yugoslavia are the only countries in Eastern Europe where people can own farms.

Poland has good farm land. There is enough rain to grow food. One third of the people are farmers. But Poland does not grow enough food. It must import food from other countries. Poland has a cool climate. Many crops cannot grow in this cool climate. Most Polish farmers work the same way people worked hundreds of years ago. They do not have enough tools and farm machines. They do not use enough fertilizer.

Poland has few natural resources. Coal is Poland's most important resource. Poland buys most of its resources from the Soviet Union.

The Communist party rules Poland. The leader of the party is Poland's leader. The Soviet Union tells Poland's leaders how to rule the country. Most of the time, Polish leaders listen to the Soviet Union.

Many Poles are not happy with their Communist government. They want more consumer goods. They also want more freedom. They want the freedom to speak against their leaders. They want more freedom to practice their religion.

All Polish workers are paid by the government. In 1980 many Polish workers were unhappy. They began to form trade unions. Most free countries have trade unions. Trade unions are organizations that help workers. Sometimes they help workers get higher wages. There are unions in the Soviet Union and Eastern Europe. But all these unions are controlled by the Communist party. Polish workers decided to start trade unions that were not controlled by the party. This was against the law.

The Poles started an organization called Solidarity. All the new trade unions were part of Solidarity. Millions of Poles joined Solidarity. They hoped the unions would bring more freedom to all of Poland.

The Soviet Communists did not like Solidarity. They did not want the Poles to have more freedom. The Soviet Communists told Polish leaders that the country could not have the new trade unions. So the Polish leaders sent the union leaders to jail for many months. People are no longer allowed to be part of Solidarity.

People wave flags at a meeting of Solidarity.

There is more freedom in Poland today that in other Communist countries. But most people want even more freedom. Many Poles would like Poland to become a democracy. This may not happen for a very long time. Right now the Communist party has strong control over Poland.

Think, Remember, Write

A. Write the Answer

Write a sentence to answer each question.

1. What is the language of Poland?

2. What sea is to the north of Poland?

142

3. What is the capital of Poland?

4. What is the most important river in Poland?

5. What is Poland's most important natural resource?

B. Finish Up

Use the words in dark print to finish each sentence. Write the words you choose on your paper.

Solidarity	**Roman Catholic**	**apartment**
privately owned	**Czechoslovakia**	**Soviet Union**

1. The _____ religion is important to most Poles.

2. Tall mountains are between _____ and Poland.

3. The _____ is to the east of Poland.

4. The government decides what size _____ a family should have.

5. Most Polish farms are _____.

6. Poles are not allowed to join _____, the organization of free trade unions in Poland.

C. Find the Answer

On your paper, copy each sentence that tells about things most Poles want. You should write 3 sentences.

1. Poles want more consumer goods.

2. Poles want the government to own the farms.

3. Poles want free trade unions.

4. Many Poles would like their country to be a democracy.

Skill Words

centimeters   kilometers   Krakow   Gdansk

A distance scale is used to show how far apart places are on a map. Some distance scales use inches to show how many miles apart places are. Other distance scales use centimeters to show how many kilometers are between places. Some maps have distance scales that show miles and kilometers.

Look at the political map of Poland on this page. The distance scale for this map shows that one inch is the same as 100 miles.

POLAND

A. Locate the Answer

Write the correct answer to each question.

1. How many inches are between Warsaw and Krakow?

   1 1/2 inches   2 inches   2 1/2 inches

2. What is the distance between Warsaw and Krakow?

   about 150 miles   about 250 miles   about 300 miles

3. How many inches are between Krakow and Gdansk?

   1 1/2 inches   2 inches   3 inches

4. What is the distance between Krakow and Gdansk?

   about 150 miles   about 250 miles   about 300 miles

5. What is the distance between Warsaw and Gdansk?

   about 50 miles   about 150 miles   about 250 miles

B. Match Up

Finish each sentence in Group A with an answer from Group B. Write the letter of the correct answer on your paper.

Group A

1. A .... is used to show how far apart places are on a map.

2. Some distance scales use .... to show how many miles apart places are.

3. Some distance scales use centimeters to show how many .... are between places.

Group B

a. inches

b. distance scale

c. kilometers

CHAPTER 20

The Communist Countries

NEW WORDS: satellites   Hungary   Romania   secret police
dictator   Warsaw Pact   Comecon   the West   free world

The Soviet Union was the only Communist country before
World War II. The Soviets fought in Eastern Europe during the
war. They captured many countries from the Germans. At last
the war ended. Thousands of American, French, and British
soldiers had fought in Europe. These soldiers went home
after the war. But Soviet soldiers did not go home. They
stayed in Eastern Europe.The countries where they stayed
became Communist countries.

Soviet soldiers invaded Hungary with tanks in 1956.

Today six countries of Eastern Europe are dominated by the Soviet Union. They are called Soviet satellites. A satellite country must obey the Soviet Union. It must be ruled by a Communist party like the one in the Soviet Union.

In 1956 the people of Hungary tried to change some of their laws. Their Communist party became less powerful. The new laws gave people more freedom. The Soviet Communists did not like these new laws. They sent their soldiers to fight in Hungary. The people of Hungary did not have the weapons they needed to fight against Soviet soldiers. The Soviets won. Soon the Communist party had control over Hungary again. The people of Eastern Europe do not want Soviet soldiers fighting in their countries. So most of the time, these countries obey the Soviet Union.

In some ways the countries of Eastern Europe are different from each other. People in Poland own their own farms. East Germany has better transportation than other countries in Eastern Europe. Romania has more trade with the United States. Each country has its own language.

The countries of Eastern Europe are alike in many ways. Every country has a secret police. Every country is ruled by a Communist party. The leader of each country is a dictator. A dictator has full power to rule and make laws. Children study the Russian language in all satellite countries of Eastern Europe.

The Soviet Union and the six countries of Eastern Europe have promised to fight for each other during a war. This promise is called the Warsaw Pact. When the Soviets fought in Hungary, five countries from the Warsaw Pact fought with them.

The Soviet Union and the countries of Eastern Europe have formed an organization. It is called Comecon. There are ten countries in Comecon. They are all ruled by Communists. A few of the countries are not in Europe. In some ways, Comecon is like the Common Market. The countries have joined together to help each other trade. Comecon countries trade mostly with each other. They decide together what the prices of goods should be. They plan how to use and share natural resources. The Soviet Union is the leader of Comecon.

In the past few years, there has been more trade between the Communist countries and the countries of the West. The countries of Western Europe and North America are sometimes called the West. The Soviet Union buys American wheat and corn. American stores sell clothing from many countries in Eastern Europe.

There are big differences between the Communist countries and the countries of the West. The countries of Western Europe and America care a lot about peace. By working together, the countries of the free world and the Communists can keep peace in the world.

American and Soviet leaders sign a treaty.

Think, Remember, Write

A. Finish Up

Use the words in dark print to finish each sentence. Write the words you choose on your paper.

satellites **West** **Comecon** **captured** **Pact**
Russian **Hungary** **Romania** **transportation**
Soviet Union **dictator** **police**

1. _____ is a country that has more trade with the West.

2. Soviet _____ are countries that obey the Soviet Union.

3. _____ is an organization that helps Communist countries have more trade with each other.

4. The countries of North America and Western Europe are sometimes called the _____.

5. In 1956 Soviet soldiers fought in _____.

6. The Soviet Union _____ countries in Eastern Europe during World War II.

7. There are secret _____ in all the countries of Eastern Europe.

8. Children study the _____ language in all satellite countries of Eastern Europe.

9. East Germany has better _____ than other countries in Eastern Europe.

10. The countries of the Warsaw _____ have promised to fight for each other during a war.

11. Before World War II, the _____ was the only Communist country.

12. Each country in Eastern Europe is ruled by a _____.

B. True or False

Write **T** for each sentence that is true. Write **F** for each sentence that is false.

1. Soviet soldiers remained in Eastern Europe after World War II.

2. American, French, and British soldiers went home after World War II.

3. Six countries of Eastern Europe are Soviet satellites.

4. In 1956 the Communist party of Hungary became less powerful.

5. In 1956 the Warsaw Pact countries did not fight with the Soviets in Hungary.

6. All the countries of Eastern and Western Europe belong to the same Common Market.

7. Comecon countries decide what the prices of goods should be.

8. Communist countries and the countries of the West do not trade with each other.

SKILL BUILDER 20: Using Latitude and Longitude on a Political Map

Skill Words

Prague   Tashkent   Yakutsk

Lines of latitude are east and west lines around the earth. Lines of longitude are north and south lines. Together lines of latitude and longitude make it easy to locate places on maps.

Lines of latitude and longitude are used to locate places on political maps. The map on the next page is a political map of Eastern Europe and the Soviet Union. What is the location of Prague in Czechoslovakia? Its latitude is 50°N, and its longitude is 14°E. We can say that Prague's location is 50°N, 14°E.

EASTERN EUROPE AND THE SOVIET UNION

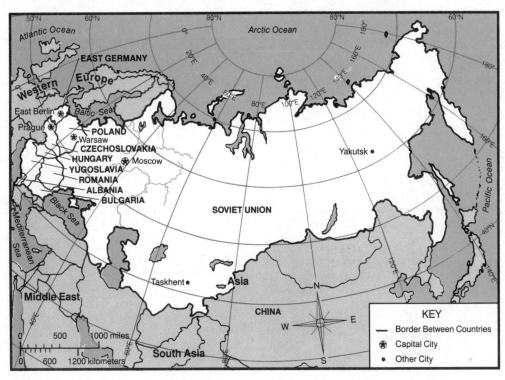

A. Match Up

Look at the political map of Eastern Europe and the Soviet Union. Use the lines of latitude and longitude to locate cities on the map. Finish each sentence in Group A with an answer from Group B. Write the letter of the correct answer on your paper.

<table>
<tr><td align="center">Group A</td><td align="center">Group B</td></tr>
<tr><td>1. The city on this map that is farthest east is ....</td><td>a. 13°E</td></tr>
<tr><td>2. The latitude and longitude of Yakutsk is ....</td><td>b. Tashkent</td></tr>
<tr><td>3. The latitude of East Berlin is 52°N. Its longitude is ....</td><td>c. 52°N, 21°E</td></tr>
<tr><td>4. The city on this map that is farthest south is ....</td><td>d. Yakutsk</td></tr>
<tr><td>5. The latitude and longitude of Tashkent is ....</td><td>e. 41°N, 69°E</td></tr>
<tr><td>6. Moscow's longitude is 37°E. Its latitude is ....</td><td>f. 62°N, 130°E</td></tr>
<tr><td>7. The latitude and longitude of Warsaw is ....</td><td>g. 55°N</td></tr>
</table>

PART 2:

Africa
Asia
Australia
the Middle East

UNIT FIVE

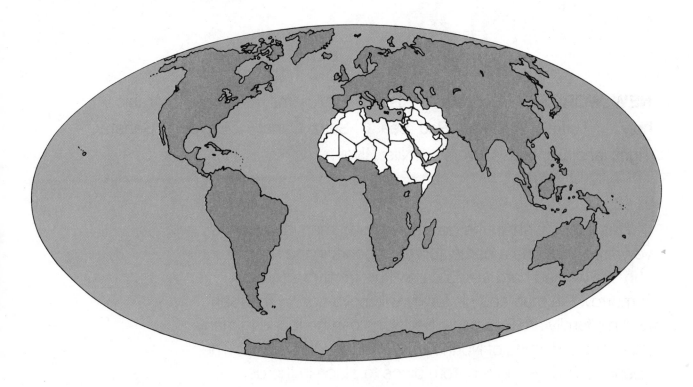

The Middle East and North Africa

You will read these chapters in Unit 5:

CHAPTER 21

Looking at the Middle East and North Africa

NEW WORDS: Bedouins   Islam   Muslims   Arabs   Arabic
holy   Turkey   Iran   Red Sea   Suez Canal   Egypt   Sahara
Tigris and Euphrates rivers   Nile River

It is late at night in the desert. A young man in his tent is very tired. He rode a camel for many hours in the hot desert sun. He worked hard taking care of his family's sheep. Tomorrow the man and his family will move again. The man and his family are Bedouins. Bedouins can be found in many parts of the deserts of North Africa and the Middle East. They spend their days moving from place to place in the desert.

Millions of people live in the Middle East and North Africa.

THE MIDDLE EAST AND NORTH AFRICA

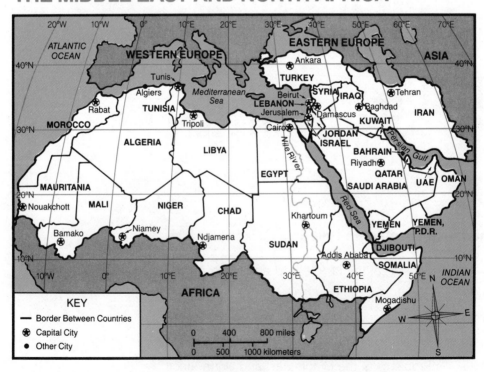

The Bedouins are a small part of the people who live in this area. Religion is very important to the people in this part of the world. Most people in this area believe in a religion called Islam. People who believe in Islam are called Muslims. There is one country in the Middle East where most people are not Muslims. That country is Israel. Most people in Israel are Jews.

A Bedouin camp near Jerusalem

Most of the people of the Middle East and North Africa are Arabs. Most Arabs speak the Arabic language. Arabic is a holy language for all Muslims. Two countries in this area are not Arab countries. These countries are Turkey and Iran. But they are Muslim countries.

Today there are more than 20 countries in the Middle East and North Africa. This part of the world is important because it is close to Asia, Europe, and Africa. It is also near important bodies of water. The Atlantic Ocean, the Mediterranean Sea, and the Red Sea are close to this area. The seas of this area are used for shipping and world trade. They are used for transportation from one continent to another.

One of the world's busiest canals is in the Middle East. It is the Suez Canal. This canal is in the country of Egypt. Ships use the Suez Canal to sail from the Mediterranean Sea to the Red Sea. The canal makes it easy for ships to sail from Europe to Asia.

A lot of land in the Middle East and North Africa is covered with deserts. The deserts are hot and dry. The Sahara is the world's largest desert. The Sahara covers most of North Africa. Sometimes there will be no rain at all for a long time in the desert. Only a small part of the population lives in the deserts of the area.

Camels are used for many jobs.

Most people of the Middle East and North Africa live near the Mediterranean coast. They also live near rivers. These areas have the best farm land. For thousands of years, people have used the waters of the Tigris and Euphrates rivers to water their fields for farming. The land near the Nile River is also used for farming. Most of the land in the Middle East and North Africa is not good farm land. A lot of food must be bought from other countries of the world. The areas that have good farm land are very crowded.

There are not many natural resources in the Middle East and North Africa. Water is a natural resource which most countries in this area need. Most countries do not get enough rain. There is not enough water for farming. There is not enough water for factory work.

Many countries in this area are rich in one natural resource. That resource is oil. Perhaps half of the world's oil is in this area. Most modern countries in other parts of the world do not have enough oil. They must buy oil from the Middle East.

An oil well being drilled in the desert

Most countries in the Middle East and North Africa are not modern. There are not many factories in the area. Many villages do not have electricity. Most farmers work the same way that farmers worked long ago. They do not use good machines or fertilizer. They are not able to grow a lot of food.

Many areas of the Middle East and North Africa do not have modern transportation. In deserts and villages, people often use camels, horses, and other animals. There are not many roads in this part of the world. In cities, there are cars and buses. Many countries have railroads between cities.

Oil has helped some countries of this area become very rich. But most people are not rich. They are very poor. Millions of people do not know how to read. Most countries do not grow enough food for their people. There have been many wars in this part of the world. Even today this area does not have peace. How do people live in this important part of the world? You will find out as you read the next chapters.

Think, Remember, Write

A. True or False

Write **T** for each sentence that is true. Write **F** for each sentence that is false.

1. Most people in the Middle East and North Africa believe in the religion called Islam.

2. The Sahara is the world's largest desert.

3. Iran and Turkey are Arab countries.

4. There is too much water in the Middle East and North Africa.

5. The Suez Canal makes it easy for ships to sail from the Mediterranean Sea to the Red Sea.

6. All the people in the Middle East are very rich.

7. Most countries in the Middle East are not modern.

B. Finish the Sentence

Write the word that finishes the sentence.

1. Some countries of the Middle East and North Africa are rich in ===.

   water   oil   gold

2. People who believe in Islam are called ===.

   Muslims   Jews   Catholics

3. Most people in the Middle East are ===.

   Russians   Americans   Arabs

4. The === River is **not** in the Middle East or North Africa.

   Nile   Tigris   Amazon

5. The Suez Canal is in ===.

   Iran   Egypt   Turkey

C. Map Study

Look at the map of the Middle East and North Africa on page 154. Write a sentence to answer each question with facts from the map.

1. Name 5 bodies of water that are on the map.

2. Which country is near the Atlantic Ocean?

3. Name 9 countries that have coasts on the Mediterranean Sea.

4. Name 5 countries that are close to the Red Sea.

159

Skill Words

resource map   minerals   copper

Resource maps show where natural resources can be found in an area. Some resource maps show where minerals are found. Minerals are oil, metals, and other resources found in the earth. Other resource maps show which crops are grown. Some maps show what factory goods are made in an area.

A map key is part of a resource map. The symbols in the map key show what resources are shown on the map.

The map on this page shows where some minerals can be found in the Middle East and North Africa. From this map we can learn that some countries are rich in oil and natural gas.

RESOURCE MAP OF THE MIDDLE EAST AND NORTH AFRICA

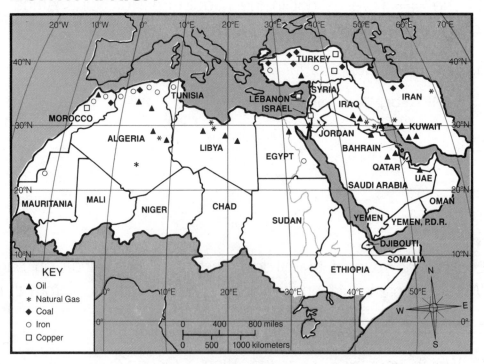

A. Locate the Answer

Look at the resource map to answer each question. Then write the correct answer to each question.

1. Which country has coal?

   Egypt   Iraq   Turkey

2. Which country does **not** have oil?

   Saudi Arabia   Chad   Iraq

3. Which country has natural gas?

   Saudi Arabia   Egypt   Iraq

4. Which country has iron?

   Turkey   Chad   Saudi Arabia

5. Which country has copper?

   Jordan   Israel   Sudan

B. Write the Answer

Write a sentence to answer each question.

1. What resources does Iran have?

2. What resources does Algeria have?

3. What are three countries on the map with no resources?

CHAPTER 22

Egypt: The Gift of the Nile

NEW WORDS: Christian Egyptians Cairo flooded soil dam Aswan High Dam floods Lake Nasser mud bricks running water

Which Arab country has the largest population? Which Arab country has land in both Africa and the Middle East? Which Arab country uses water from the Nile River to water the fields for farming? The answer to all these questions is Egypt.

EGYPT

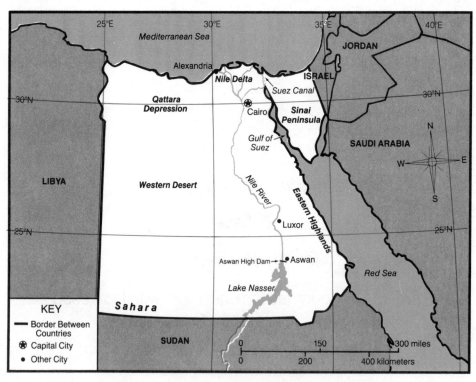

Egypt has about 46 million people. It has more people than any other Arab country. Like other Arab countries, most of the people are Muslims. A small part of the population is Christian. The people of Egypt are called Egyptians. Arabic is

the official language of Egypt. The population of Egypt is growing very fast. Most Egyptian families are very large. Most Egyptians are very poor. About half the people of Egypt live in cities. The cities are near the Nile. Cairo is the largest city. It is also the capital of Egypt.

Cairo is the largest city in Egypt.

The Nile River is very important to Egypt. The Nile River starts in a country far to the south of Egypt. It goes from the south to the north of Egypt. The river ends at the Mediterranean Sea.

Egypt is a hot, dry country. It needs water from the Nile. Egypt needs this water because it gets very little rain. Most of Egypt is dry deserts. For thousands of years, Egyptians have lived on land near the Nile. Cities were built near the Nile. Today few people live in Egypt's huge deserts. The land near the Nile is very crowded.

How has the Nile helped Egypt? Every summer, for thousands of years, the Nile River flooded the land around it. Rich soil was in this river water. Every year the land near the Nile got new soil. This new soil was very good for farming.

The Egyptians built a huge dam on the Nile River. It is called the Aswan High Dam. The Aswan High Dam has stopped the floods of the Nile River. Now the land near the river does not get new soil every year. Farmers must buy fertilizers to use on the soil.

The Aswan High Dam has helped Egypt. The dam saves Nile water in a large lake. It is called Lake Nasser. Water from the lake can be used to water fields all year long. Egypt now has more land that can be used for farming than it had before the dam was built. The dam also uses water power to make electricity. Half of Egypt's electricity comes from the Aswan High Dam.

The Aswan High Dam on the Nile River

Egypt has few natural resources. But the country does have oil in its deserts. This oil is sold to other countries. Egypt is not an industrial country. It does not have a lot of factories. Egyptians are trying to start new industries.

Water from Lake Nasser is used to irrigate farm lands.

Millions of Egyptians are farmers. They work the way farmers worked long ago. They do not have modern tools and machines. These farmers work on small farms. They work very hard for many hours each day. But they do not grow enough food for the people of Egypt. Egypt buys almost half of its food from other countries.

Egyptian farmers live in villages. They live in small houses made of mud bricks. Most homes do not have electricity. Most homes do not have running water. Women must carry water to their homes each day.

More than half the people of Egypt do not know how to read and write. The government is trying to help its people learn to read. It has built many new schools. The law says all children must go to school for six years. But there are not enough schools. Many children must work to help their families.

Egypt is a leading country in the Middle East today. But it is a country with many problems. The land near the Nile is very crowded. Egypt needs more farm land. Farmers must learn modern ways to grow more food. Egypt needs more factories. The people need more schools for their children. The Egyptians are working on their problems. They want their country to be a great leader in the Arab world.

Think, Remember, Write

A. Finish Up

Use the words in dark print to finish each sentence. Write the words you choose on your paper.

population   **Aswan High Dam**   **Arabic**
     Lake Nasser   **Islam**

1. Most Egyptians believe in the religion of _____.

2. Egypt's official language is _____.

3. Egypt's _____ is growing very fast.

4. Nile River water is saved in _____.

5. Egyptians built the _____ to stop the flooding of the Nile.

B. Write the Answer

Write a sentence to answer each question.

1. How many people live in Egypt?

2. What are the people of Egypt called?

3. What did the Nile River do every summer?

4. What is Egypt's capital?

5. What problems does Egypt have today? Write 2 sentences.

C. Match Up

Finish each sentence in Group A with an answer from Group B. Write the letter of the correct answer on your paper.

<u>Group A</u>

1. Most of the land in Egypt is

   _____.

2. Every year the Nile River gave Egypt _____.

3. The Aswan High Dam makes

   _____.

4. More than half of the people do not know _____.

5. Egyptian law says all children must _____.

<u>Group B</u>

a. new soil that was good for farming

b. go to school for six years

c. hot, dry desert

d. half of Egypt's electricity

e. how to read and write

Skill Words

> relief map   highlands   Qattara Depression

Most countries have several kinds of land. Some places have low plains. Other areas have tall mountains. A relief map helps you learn about the kind of land a country has. Relief maps show where the country has highlands. Highlands are lands high above sea level. Relief maps show where the land has mountains, low plains, and plateaus.

A map key is part of a relief map. The symbols in the map key show different kinds of land on a relief map.

RELIEF MAP OF EGYPT

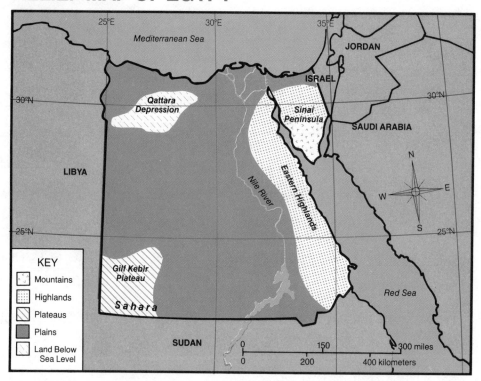

A. Locate the Answer

Look at the relief map to answer each question. Then write the correct answer to each question.

1. What kind of land is near the Nile River?

   plains   mountains   highlands

2. What kind of land is at the Qattara Depression?

   plateaus   mountains   land below sea level

3. Which part of Egypt has mountains?

   Qattara Depression   Sinai Peninsula   land near the Nile

4. What kind of land is near the Red Sea?

   plains   land below sea level   highlands

5. What kind of land is in southwest Egypt?

   plains   plateaus   mountains

B. Write the Answer

Write a sentence to answer each question.

1. What does a relief map help you learn?

2. What are highlands?

3. What do symbols show on a relief map?

CHAPTER 23

Israel: A Jewish Country

NEW WORDS: kibbutz   Israelis   Hebrew   Sea of Galilee
Negev Desert   Jerusalem   Tel Aviv   Dead Sea   salty
grapefruit   Palestinians   taxes   costly

Night has come to a kibbutz farm in Israel. All the
children are asleep in a children's house. On this kibbutz in

ISRAEL

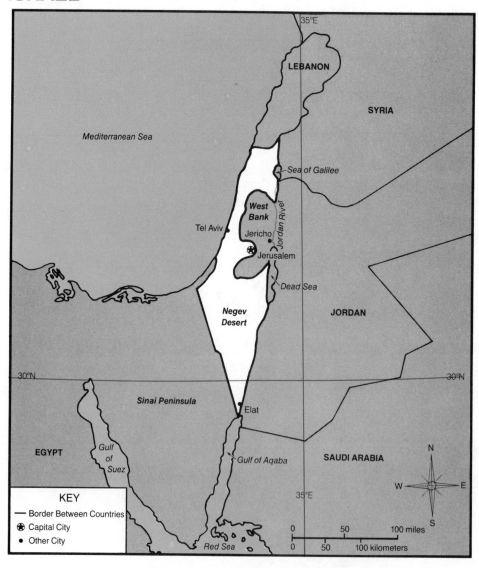

Israel, children live and play in a children's house. They see their parents often, but they do not live with them. Most kibbutz children think the children's house is a good place to live.

Israel is the only country in the world with kibbutz farms. A kibbutz is owned by all of its members. They share the work on the farm. People do not get paid for their work. But the kibbutz gives its members the things they need. There are schools and doctors. Often there is a factory. Members vote for kibbutz leaders. Everyone eats together in a large dining room. The members feel that they are part of a very large family. Only a small part of Israel's people lives on kibbutz farms. But these people grow half of Israel's food.

The people of Israel are called Israelis. There are four million Israelis. Hebrew and Arabic are the official languages. Most Israelis are Jews. But there are also thousands of Israeli Arabs. The Arabs are Muslims and Christians. The laws allow all these groups to practice their religions.

Children on an Israeli kibbutz

Israel is a small country in the Middle East. It is at the eastern end of the Mediterranean Sea. There are plains near the Mediterranean Sea. Most of Israel's people live on plains near the coast. The best farm land is in the northern half of the country. An important lake is in the north. It is called the Sea of Galilee. This lake water is used to water the fields for farming.

The southern part of Israel is a dry desert. It is called the Negev Desert. Israelis have built farms and cities in the desert. They built pipes to carry water from the Sea of Galilee to the Negev. Israelis use this water in desert farms and cities.

Jerusalem is the capital of Israel. It is Israel's most important city. It is a holy city to many people of the world. There are places in Jerusalem that are holy to Christians, Muslims, and Jews. Tel Aviv is the largest city in Israel. It is on the Mediterranean Sea. Many factories and businesses are near Tel Aviv.

Jerusalem is a holy city to many people around the world.

The Dead Sea is a salt water lake in Israel. It is the lowest place on the earth. The water is so salty that fish and plants cannot live in it.

Life in Israel is very different from life in other countries in the area. Most people in Israel know how to read and write. There are free schools for all children. Most people live in cities. Farmers use modern machines and fertilizer. Israel is a democracy. Arabs and Jews vote for people to work for them in Israel's Parliament.

Israel has very few natural resources. It must buy all of its oil from other countries. It buys raw materials from other countries. The Israelis have worked hard to build a modern country. Today Israeli factories make many goods. Israeli farmers grow most of the food they need. Israel exports food to other countries. Oranges, grapefruit, and flowers from Israel are sold in many countries.

Why is Israel the only Jewish country in the Middle East? Thousands of years ago, the Jews ruled this land. Then the land was taken over by other peoples. Most Jews had to move to other countries. Many Arabs came to live in this land. Some Jews remained there too.

During World War II, millions of European Jews were killed by the leaders of Germany. After the war, many Jews needed a home. They wanted the land of Israel to be their home again. In 1948 the country of Israel was formed.

A large group of Arabs in Israel left when the new Jewish country was formed. These Arabs are called Palestinians. They do not have a country now. There has been fighting between the Israelis and the Palestinians over the land.

Fighting and wars have been a big problem for Israel. Since 1948, the Arab countries have fought four wars against Israel. Each time Israel has remained free. Israel now has land that it took from the Arabs during a war in 1967. Egypt is the only Arab country that has made peace with Israel.

Israel has other problems too. Israel must have a large, strong army. The country buys many weapons. Israelis must pay very high taxes to pay for their army. The country also imports more goods than it sells to other countries. Almost everything in Israel has become very costly. Many people are unhappy with the high taxes and high prices.

Every year thousands of people visit Israel. They visit holy places in Jerusalem. They swim at Israel's warm beaches. Some people visit or work on a kibbutz. Visitors see that Israelis are proud of their modern country.

Think, Remember, Write

A. Find the Answer

On your paper, copy each sentence that tells about Israel. You should write 4 sentences.

1. A kibbutz is owned by all its members.

2. On most kibbutz farms, children live in a children's house.

3. Few Israelis live near the Mediterranean Sea.

4. Many factories are near Tel Aviv.

5. Israelis use water from the Sea of Galilee to water their fields for farming.

6. Most people in Israel do not know how to read and write.

B. True or False

Write **T** for each sentence that is true. Write **F** for each sentence that is false.

1. Israel is rich in natural resources.

2. Israel is a democracy.

3. Israeli farmers do not use modern machines or fertilizers.

4. After World War II, Jews wanted Israel to be their home again.

5. Palestinians are Arabs who left Israel in 1948.

6. There is peace between Israel and all the Arab countries.

7. Israelis pay very low taxes.

8. Most things in Israel are very costly.

C. Write the Answer

Write a sentence to answer each question.

1. What are the people of Israel called?

2. What are the two official languages of Israel?

3. What is Israel's capital?

4. What is the lowest place on the earth?

SKILL BUILDER 23: Using a Climate Map

Skill Words

climate map	Mediterranean climate	mild
desert climate	season	Elat

Climate maps help you learn about the weather in an area. They show which areas are rainy and which areas are dry. Climate maps help you learn which places are hot and which are cold.

The map key on the climate map on page 176 shows two different climates. The desert climate has hot summers, mild winters, and almost no rain. A Mediterranean climate has hot, dry summers and cool, rainy winters.

A. True or False

Look at the climate map. Then write **T** for each sentence that is true. Write **F** for each sentence that is false.

1. The land in northern Israel has a Mediterranean climate.

2. The city of Tel Aviv has a desert climate.

3. The city of Elat has rainy winters.

4. The city of Jerusalem has a desert climate.

5. The land near the Sea of Galilee has hot, dry summers and cool, wet winters.

CLIMATE MAP OF ISRAEL

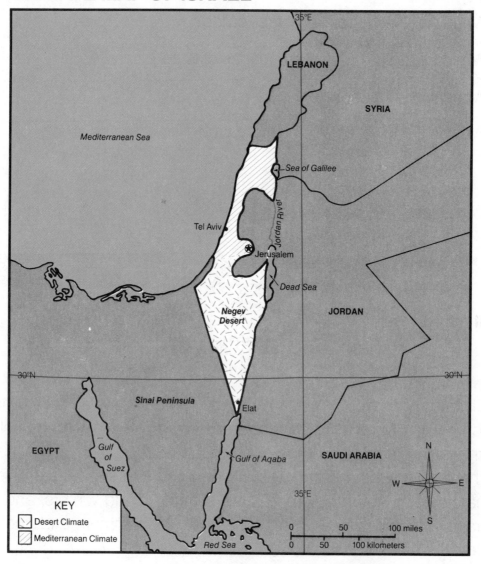

176

CHAPTER 24

Other Countries of the Middle East

NEW WORDS: Fatima   Saudi Arabia   veil   Naila   scarf
Mecca   Islamic Republic   Farsi   Persian carpets   Turks
Turkish   Syria   Syrian   Damascus

Fatima   is a Muslim woman in Saudi Arabia. She wears
a long dress that almost reaches the ground. Her face and
hair are covered with a black veil. Naila is a Muslim woman in
Turkey. Naila wears a scarf to cover her hair. But she does
not cover her face with a veil. Fatima and Naila are two
women in the Middle East. They are both Muslims. But there
are big differences between their countries.

Muslim women in Iran

Women are thought to be less important than men in most of the Middle East. More Muslim boys go to school than girls. In many countries, women are not allowed to vote. Most Muslim women do not work at jobs outside their homes. The religion of the Muslims allows men to have four wives. Many Muslims believe that women should be seen only by their families. This is why many women cover their hair and faces when they leave their homes.

Saudi Arabia is the richest country in the Middle East today. This Arab country has huge amounts of oil. Saudi Arabia sells oil to many countries of the world.

Saudi Arabia is a desert country. The weather is hot most of the time. There is only a small amount of good farm land in Saudi Arabia. There are no lakes or rivers in Saudi Arabia.

Islam began in Saudi Arabia. The city of Mecca is in Saudi Arabia. It is a holy city for all Muslims. All Muslims must try to visit Mecca once during their lives. Every year Muslims from every part of the world visit Mecca. Today the laws of Islam are the laws of Saudi Arabia. The country is ruled by a king. The king is very powerful.

Saudi women have less freedom than men. Saudi women must wear veils when they leave their homes. They are not allowed to drive cars. They are not allowed to work at most jobs.

Today Saudi Arabia is using its oil money to become a modern country. Most people in this country do not know how to read and write. The government is building schools, roads, and hospitals. It is trying to start new industries.

Iran is another country that is ruled by the laws of Islam. Iran is called an Islamic Republic. It is ruled by a religious leader. Like Saudi Arabia, women must cover their faces when they leave their homes. Iran is also rich in oil.

There are differences between Iran and Saudi Arabia. Iran has more people. The people of Iran are not Arabs. They have not fought in wars against Israel. The people speak a language called Farsi.

There are many mountains and plateaus in Iran. Iran has deserts too. There are hot summers and very cold winters. There is not enough good farm land. Iran must import food.

Iran has more industries than Saudi Arabia. Factories make steel and clothing. Beautiful Persian carpets are made in this country.

Turkey is another country in the Middle East. The people are called Turks. They speak the Turkish language. Most Turks are Muslims, but they are not Arabs. Turkey has not fought against Israel.

Turkey is in the northern part of the Middle East. The western part of Turkey is in Europe. The eastern part is in Asia. There are many mountains in Turkey. This country is not rich in oil. It has good farm land. More than half the people are farmers. Turkey grows more food than it needs. It sells food to other countries.

This farmer lives in the part of Turkey called Anatolia.

Turkey has been trying to become a modern country. Many schools have been built. Now more than two thirds of the people know how to read. But more schools are needed. Turkish women no longer wear face veils.

The country of Syria has been a leader in the wars against Israel. The Soviet Union has given Syria many weapons for these wars. Most people in this Arab country are Muslims. The people speak Arabic. Most Syrian women do not wear face veils. Most children know how to read.

Damascus is the capital city of Syria. It is the oldest city in the world. Some parts of Damascus have modern, new buildings. Syria has more farm land than most countries in the area. Part of this country is covered with a large desert.

The countries of the Middle East are different from each other. The religion of Islam joins people of the area together. The people also share many problems. In Chapter 25, you will learn how the people are trying to solve their problems.

Damascus, Syria, is the oldest city in the world.

Think, Remember, Write

A. Finish Up

Use the words in dark print to finish each sentence. Write the words you choose on your paper.

Turkey   Saudi Arabia   Persian carpets
Syria   Iran

1. _____ is the richest country in the Middle East.

2. Saudi Arabia and _____ are ruled by the laws of Islam.

3. Beautiful _____ are made in Iran.

4. _____ grows more food than it needs.

5. _____ has been a leader in the wars against Israel.

B. Write It Right

The words in the sentences below are mixed up. Write each sentence correctly.

1. Arabia Saudi a is country. desert

2. speak Farsi. a language people The Iran of called

3. of Turkey in Europe. is part western The

4. eastern The part Turkey of Asia. in is

C. Match Up

Finish each sentence in Group A with a word from Group B. Write the letter of the correct word on your paper.

<u>Group A</u>

1. Some Muslim women cover their faces with _____ when they leave home.

2. Iran's government is called an _____ Republic.

3. The capital of Syria is _____.

4. The religion of the Muslims allows men to have four _____.

5. Saudi Arabia and _____ are rich in oil.

6. Many _____ in the Middle East do not have schools or electricity.

7. _____ gets many weapons from the Soviet Union.

8. _____ Arabia is a desert country with little farm land.

9. All Muslims must try to visit the city of _____ once during their lives.

<u>Group B</u>

a. Damascus

b. Iran

c. veils

d. Islamic

e. wives

f. villages

g. Mecca

h. Saudi

i. Syria

SKILL BUILDER 24: Comparing a Climate Map With a Political Map

Skill Words

steppes climate

We can learn things about a country by studying two kinds of maps of that country. This page has a political map and a climate map of Syria. Look at the southeast part of Syria on both maps. The political map does not show cities in the southeast part of Syria. The climate map shows us that this part of Syria has a desert climate. From these maps we learn that Syrians have not built cities where there is a desert climate.

The map also shows a steppes climate. A steppes climate has a hot, dry season for most of the year. Winters are cold, with a little rain.

POLITICAL MAP OF SYRIA   CLIMATE MAP OF SYRIA

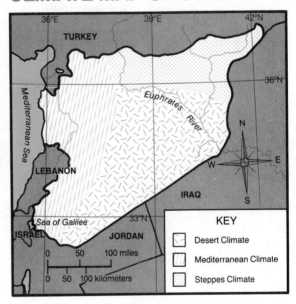

A. Finish Up

Read each sentence and look at both maps of Syria. Use the words in dark print to finish each sentence. Write the words you choose on your paper.

Mediterranean   **rivers**   **steppes**
Damascus   **desert**

1. The city of .... has a Mediterranean climate.

2. Most cities are near .... in a steppes climate.

3. Northeastern Syria has a .... climate.

4. There is empty land in Syria's ....

5. From these two maps we learn that Syrians built cities in places with a .... climate or near rivers.

CHAPTER 25

Problems of the Middle East and North Africa

NEW WORDS: Latin alphabet   irrigation   sea water   fresh water   desalting plant   Kuwait   used up   lack   Iraq   Lebanon   armies

For hundreds of years, the Muslim men of Turkey were allowed to have four wives. They wrote their Turkish language with Arabic letters. The leaders of Turkey wanted their country to become a modern country. They made new laws to help their country change. Today Turkish men can have only one wife. Turkish women are allowed to vote. Turks now use the Latin alphabet. But the people in Turkish villages still live by the old ways. Turkey must do a lot more work to become a modern country.

Children going to school in Istanbul, Turkey.

Most of the countries of the Middle East and North Africa follow old ways of living. They face problems as they try to become modern countries. One big problem is illiteracy. In many countries, more than half the people do not know how to read and write. These people cannot do the kind of work needed to build modern countries. In most countries, families are very large. It is hard for parents to feed their large families. There are not enough schools for all the children. Many times children cannot go to school because they must go to work for their families.

There is not enough good farm land in the Middle East and North Africa. Most people in this area are farmers. But only a small part of the land can be used to grow crops. Most countries do not grow enough food. They must import food.

There is not enough water in the Middle East and North Africa. This is a big problem. Most countries do not get enough rain. Do you remember that Egyptians built the Aswan High Dam? You learned that the dam saves river water in Lake Nasser. The people can use this water when they need it.

In many places, people must use irrigation to grow food. Irrigation means using water from rivers and lakes to water fields when there is not enough rain. Irrigation can change deserts into farm land. In Chapter 23, you learned that pipes in Israel bring water from the Sea of Galilee to the Negev Desert. This changed parts of the desert into farm land. Most places in the Middle East and North Africa do not use irrigation. Sometimes animals are used to carry river water to dry land. This area needs better irrigation. Then there will be more farm land and more food.

Some countries are using another way to get more water. The countries of this area are close to many seas. Sea water is salty. It is not good for farming or factory work. Water without salt is called fresh water. People can take the salt out of sea water. This job is done in a desalting plant. A desalting plant changes sea water into fresh water. This fresh water is good for people, farms, and factory work. Today there is a large desalting plant in Kuwait. This oil-rich country is near Saudi Arabia. The desalting plant is helping Kuwait get the water it needs.

Some countries in this area have become rich by selling their oil to other countries. Many people believe that one day this oil will be used up. How will these countries get money when they no longer have oil to sell? The countries want to become industrial countries. Israel is the only industrial country of the area. The other countries want more factories. They want to make factory goods they can sell to other countries.

A big problem in the Middle East is the lack of peace. The Arabs and Israelis have not made peace. There has been a war between the countries of Iran and Iraq. There has been a lot of fighting in the country of Lebanon. Every year people are killed in fighting in this area. War is costly. People are spending lots of money on weapons and armies. This money could be used to build schools. More money could be used to build new factories and desalting plants.

Fighting in the streets of Beirut, Lebanon

Most children of this area have better lives today than their grandparents had. There are more schools, more factories, and more doctors. More roads are being built. Most people have enough food to eat. Some countries have been using their oil money to become more modern. The Middle East and North Africa need to find a way to have peace.

Think, Remember, Write

A. Find the Answer

On your paper, copy the sentences that tell about the problems in the Middle East and North Africa. You should write 4 sentences.

1. Illiteracy is a big problem in the Middle East and North Africa.

2. There are too many industrial countries in the area.

3. There is not enough farm land.

4. Most places do not have modern irrigation.

5. There is not enough water.

6. There are many desalting plants in every country.

7. All the oil has been used up.

B. Finish the Sentence

Write the word that finishes the sentence.

1. Most people in the Middle East are ＝＝.

    farmers   factory workers   teachers

2. The countries need modern ＝＝ to make more farm land and grow more food.

    irrigation   armies   factories

3. Salt water can be changed into fresh water in a ═══.

  hospital   irrigation   desalting plant

4. There is a large desalting plant in ═══.

  Syria   Kuwait   Turkey

C. Match Up

Finish each sentence in Group A with an answer from Group B. Write the letter of the correct answer on your paper.

Group A	Group B
1. Most countries must ‐‐‐‐‐‐‐‐‐	a. used up
2. Israel brings water from the Sea of Galilee to ‐‐‐‐‐‐‐‐‐	b. Lebanon
3. Many people believe that one day the oil will be ‐‐‐‐‐‐‐‐‐	c. import food
4. There has been fighting between Iran and ‐‐‐‐‐‐‐‐‐	d. the Negev
5. There has been fighting among the people of ‐‐‐‐‐‐‐‐‐	e. Iraq

SKILL BUILDER 25: Comparing Relief Maps to Learn About Two Countries

Skill Words

Thrace   Anatolia   central

Relief maps help you learn about the kind of land a country has. You can learn facts about two countries by comparing their relief maps.

Look at the relief maps of Saudi Arabia and Turkey on this page. These maps show differences between the two countries. Turkey has two parts. The European Turkey is called Thrace. The Asian part of Turkey is called Anatolia. All of Thrace is covered with plains. Only a small part of Anatolia has plains. We can see that there are more plains in Saudi Arabia than in Anatolia. What other facts can you learn by looking at the two maps on this page?

RELIEF MAP OF TURKEY

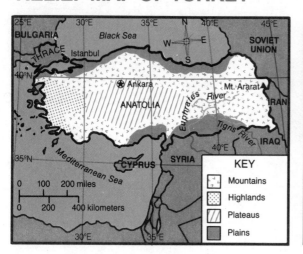

RELIEF MAP OF SAUDI ARABIA

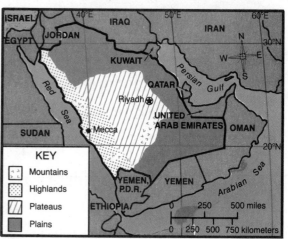

A. Turkey or Saudi Arabia?

Look at both maps. Then finish each sentence with the word **Turkey** or **Saudi Arabia**.

1. Eastern _____ has lots of mountains.

2. Eastern _____ has large areas of plains.

3. There are no rivers on the map of _____.

4. The western part of _____ is highlands and mountains.

5. Of the two countries, _____ has more mountains.

UNIT SIX

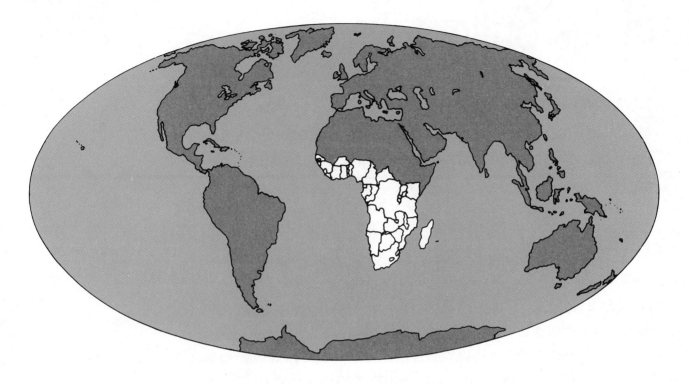

Tropical and Southern Africa

You will read these chapters in Unit 6:

CHAPTER 26

Looking at Africa South of the Sahara

NEW WORDS: diamonds   tropical   tropics   narrow
Mount Kilimanjaro   smooth   Kalahari Desert   savannas
Republic of South Africa   ethnic group   culture
cash crops   cocoa   palm oil

Which continent has most of the world's diamonds? Which one has lots of gold? Which one has millions of poor people who do not know how to read? The answer to all these questions is Africa.

Africa is very rich in natural resources. Africa has diamonds and gold. It has many kinds of metals. Africa has many

TROPICAL AND SOUTHERN AFRICA

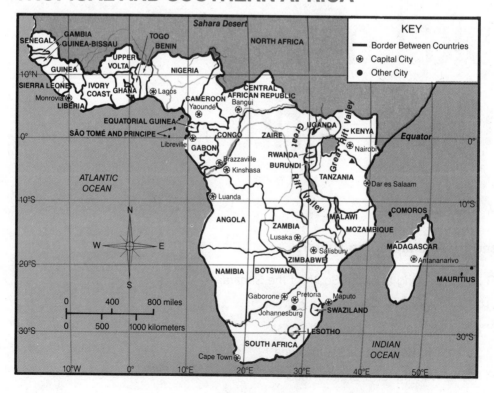

forests. There is lots of water power. But most Africans are very poor. Why are the people poor when there are so many natural resources? You will find the answers as you read this unit.

The desert named the Sahara divides Africa into two parts. One part is North Africa. The other part is the land that is south of the Sahara. This part is called Tropical and Southern Africa.

Tropical land is hot most days of the year. It is in a part of the world called the tropics. This is land near the Equator. Most of Africa is in the tropics. Most of Africa is hot. The southern part of Africa is not in the tropics. Southern Africa is cooler than Tropical Africa.

There are narrow plains near Africa's coast. Then the land rises into plateaus. Most of Africa is covered with a large plateau. It becomes higher in eastern Africa. Africa's weather is cooler where there are mountains and high plateaus.

Africa does not have long mountain chains. But there are some mountains. Mount Kilimanjaro is the highest mountain in Africa. It is not far from the Equator. But the air is cold at the top of this mountain. The air is cold because the mountain is so tall.

Africa is between two oceans. The Atlantic Ocean is to the west. The Indian Ocean is to the east. Africa has a very smooth coast. There are not many harbors and ports. This has made it hard for Africans to use the seas for trading.

There are many kinds of land in Tropical and Southern Africa. There are rain forests near the Equator. These forests are very hot and wet. There is less rain farther away from the Equator. The Kalahari Desert is a large desert in the southern part of Africa. A large part of Africa is covered with savannas. Savannas are grass-covered plains.

Who are the people of Tropical and Southern Africa? Most Africans are black people. There are small groups of Asians and Arabs. There are also some white people of European descent. The largest group of white people is in the Republic of South Africa.

Most Africans in Tropical and Southern Africa are black people.

The black people of Africa come from many ethnic groups. Each group has its own leader. Each group has its own culture. It has its own language. There are more than 800 languages spoken in Africa. Each country has many ethnic groups.

In most African countries, the people are very poor. They work on small farms. There are some very large farms in Africa too. Cash crops are grown on these farms. Cash crops are crops that can be sold to earn money. Coffee, tea, cocoa, and palm oil are African cash crops. Africans sell these cash crops to other countries.

Mining is important in Africa. Africans sell metals from their mines to many countries. There are few factories in Africa today. African leaders know their countries need more factories. They need to make goods with their raw materials. Africans could use these goods instead of buying costly imported goods. Africans could also sell goods to other countries. This would bring more money into Africa.

Transportation is poor in most of Africa. There are not many roads or railroads. Poor transportation makes it hard for African countries to trade with each other. It is also hard to send goods to other lands.

For hundreds of years, Britain, France, and other countries in Europe ruled most of Africa. Today most African countries are free. The new African countries are trying to become strong, modern countries.

Think, Remember, Write

A. Finish the Sentence

Write the word that finishes the sentence.

1. Most of Africa is ═══ .

   cold   hot   snowy

2. Most of Africa is covered with ═══ .

   plateaus   low plains   mountains

3. Most people who live in Africa south of the Sahara are ═══ .

   Asians   blacks   whites

4. The people of Africa belong to more than 800 ═══ .

   ethnic groups   countries   villages

5. Africa sells ═══ to many countries.

   cars   hats   metals

B. Write It Right

The words in the sentences below are mixed up. Write each sentence correctly.

1. grass-covered plains. Savannas are

2. crops are Cash crops earn money. are sold to that

3. important Africa. Mining in is

4. makes it hard with each other. Poor transportation to trade for African countries

5. more need factories. African countries

C. Match Up

Finish each sentence in Group A with an answer from Group B. Write the letter of the correct answer on your paper.

<u>Group A</u>

1. The tallest mountain in Africa is _____.

2. Africa gets a lot of rain near the _____.

3. A large desert in southern Africa is the _____.

4. A lot of African land is covered with _____.

5. Coffee, tea, cocoa, and palm oil are African _____.

<u>Group B</u>

a. Mount Kilimanjaro

b. cash crops

c. savannas

d. Kalahari Desert

e. Equator

Skill Words

picture graph   Kenya   Nigeria   South Africa

Graphs help us compare facts. A picture graph is one kind of graph. Picture graphs use symbols to show numbers of things. Car symbols are used in the graph on this page. Each car symbol stands for 100,000 cars.

The graph shows one car symbol and part of another car symbol for Kenya. The part of a car symbol means there are less than 100,000 cars. The symbols on the graph next to Kenya tell us that this African country has about 115,000 cars.

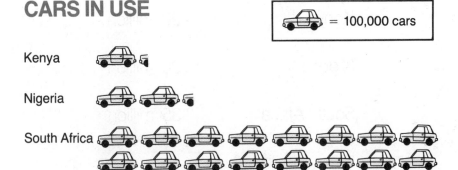

CARS IN USE

= 100,000 cars

A. Locate the Answer

Look at the graph. Then write the correct answer to each question.

1. How many cars are in Nigeria?

   115,000   215,000   2,500,000

2. How many cars are in South Africa?

   115,000   215,000   2,500,000

3. Which country has the fewest cars?

Kenya   Nigeria   South Africa

4. Which country has the most cars?

Kenya   Nigeria   South Africa

B. Make a Picture Graph

Use the numbers below to make a picture graph. Your graph will show about how many people live in Kenya, Nigeria, and South Africa.

= 10 million people

Populations

Kenya	20 million
Nigeria	90 million
South Africa	35 million

CHAPTER 27

Nigeria: A Country in the West

NEW WORDS: Nigerians   traditional religions   independent
Gulf of Guinea   swamp   streams   Niger River   Lagos
overcrowded   peanuts

Nigeria has more people than any other country in
Africa. It is the only oil-rich country that is south of the Sahara.
Nigeria is a very important African country. It is important
because it has oil and a very large population.

There are about 90 million people in Nigeria. The people
of Nigeria are called Nigerians. Almost half of the people are

NIGERIA

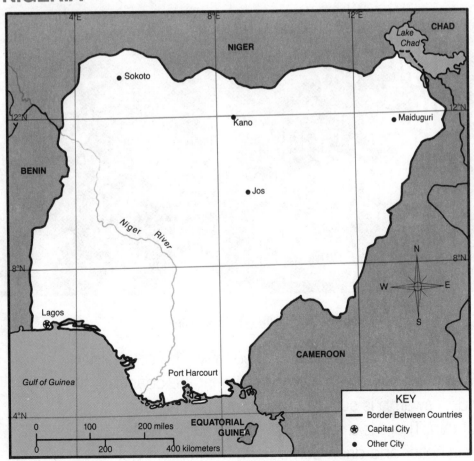

Muslims. Most Muslims live in the north. About one third of the people are Christians. Most Christians live in the south. Other Nigerians follow traditional African religions.

Most Nigerians are black Africans. They belong to many ethnic groups. There are more than 250 ethnic groups. More than 250 different languages are spoken. It is hard for Nigerians to feel that they are part of one country. It is hard to feel like one country because so many different languages are spoken.

Nigeria is one of the many African countries that was ruled by Britain. Nigeria became an independent country in 1960. English is the official language in Nigeria. English is the language used in Nigerian schools.

English is used in the schools of Nigeria.

Nigeria is in western Africa. It is a hot country. The southern part is near the Gulf of Guinea. Some land near the coast is swamp land. A swamp is soft, wet land. Southern Nigeria gets a lot of rain. There is a rain forest in the south. The land in the north is hotter and drier. Some parts of the north get almost no rain. Much of Nigeria is a plateau. Savannas cover this plateau.

There are many rivers and streams in Nigeria. The Niger River is the third largest river in Africa. The country also has lakes. Nigerians get a lot of fish from their rivers, streams, and lakes.

Lagos is the largest city in Nigeria. It is a port on the Gulf of Guinea. Lagos is Nigeria's capital. Each year many poor people leave their villages and move to Lagos. Lagos and other cities are becoming very overcrowded.

The number of people in Lagos is growing very fast.

Most Nigerians are farmers. They live in small villages. Most Nigerians do not use modern tools. They do not use fertilizers. Nigerians most often grow enough food for their country. Nigeria exports some cash crops. Cocoa, cotton, palm oil, and peanuts are sold to other countries.

Nigeria has natural resources. It has gold, coal, iron, and natural gas. It also has forests. But oil is the country's most important natural resource.

Nigeria earns most of its money by selling oil to other countries. Nigeria sells oil to the United States and to Western Europe. Nigeria has lots of oil near its southern coast. Today many Nigerians work in the country's oil fields.

Nigeria is not an industrial country. But the country is using its oil money to build new factories. Nigeria has started to use its coal and iron to make steel. It also has factories that make clothing, chemicals, food products, and other things.

Nigeria has many problems today. Only one third of the people know how to read. There are not enough schools for the children. Many people do not have jobs. The cities are overcrowded. There are not enough factories. Most people are very poor.

The leaders of Nigeria want their country to be a leader in Africa. They are using oil money to build schools, roads, and factories. Nigeria's leaders are using oil money to solve their country's problems.

Think, Remember, Write

A. Write the Answer

Write a sentence to answer each question.

1. What city is the capital of Nigeria?

2. How many people live in Nigeria?

3. How many ethnic groups are in Nigeria?

4. What country ruled Nigeria before 1960?

5. What is Nigeria's official language?

6. What cash crops does Nigeria export?

B. True or False

Write **T** for each sentence that is true. Write **F** for each sentence that is false.

1. More than 250 languages are spoken in Nigeria.

2. About half of Nigeria's people are Muslims.

3. Most Nigerians are farmers.

4. Nigerians most often grow enough food for their country.

5. Nigeria's southern part is near the Gulf of Guinea.

6. The land in northern Nigeria is a swamp.

7. Much of Nigeria is a plateau.

8. Lagos is an overcrowded city.

9. Oil is Nigeria's most important natural resource.

10. Nigeria earns most of its money by selling oil.

11. Everyone in Nigeria knows how to read.

12. Nigeria is not an independent country.

C. Finish Up

Use the words in dark print to finish each sentence. Write the words you choose on your paper.

Muslims   **swamp**   **Lagos**   **overcrowded**

Guinea   **ethnic**   **independent**   **Britain**

1. _____ is the largest city in Nigeria.

2. About half of the people in Nigeria are _____.

3. Nigeria is one of the many African countries that was ruled by _____

4. Nigeria became an _____ country in 1960.

5. A _____ is soft, wet land.

6. There are about 250 _____ groups in Nigeria.

7. The southern part of Nigeria is near the Gulf of _____.

8. Lagos and other cities are becoming _____.

SKILL BUILDER 27: Understanding Bar Graphs

Skill Words

estimate

Bar graphs are used to compare facts. The bar graph on page 205 compares the number of people in Nigeria's religious groups. Look at the bar for traditional religions. The bar stops before the line for 20 million. We can estimate that about 19 million Nigerians follow traditional African religions. Look at all three bars on the graph. Can you tell which is the largest religious group in Nigeria?

NIGERIAN RELIGIOUS GROUPS

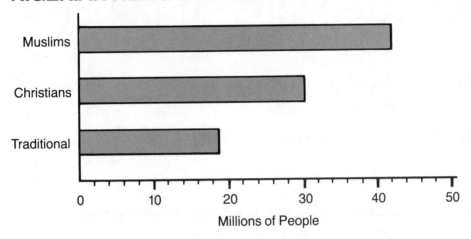

A. Finish the Sentence

Look at the bar graph. Then write the word that finishes the sentence.

1. There are ▬▬ Muslims in Nigeria.

   42 million   30 million   17 million

2. There are ▬▬ Christians in Nigeria.

   42 million   30 million   17 million

3. The ▬▬ are the largest religious group in Nigeria.

   Muslims   Christians   traditional religions

4. People who follow ▬▬ are the smallest religious group in Nigeria.

   traditional religions   Islam   Christianity

CHAPTER 28

Kenya: A Country in the East

NEW WORDS: Mombasa   coastal plains   Lake Victoria
Nairobi   Great Rift Valley   valleys   Kenyans   Swahili
developing country   oil refineries   refined

Kenya is an African country that does not have gold and diamonds. It does not have oil. It does not have coal or iron. How does this African country earn the money it needs?

Kenya is a country in eastern Africa. Kenya has a port city on the ocean. It is the city of Mombasa. Mombasa is on the

KENYA

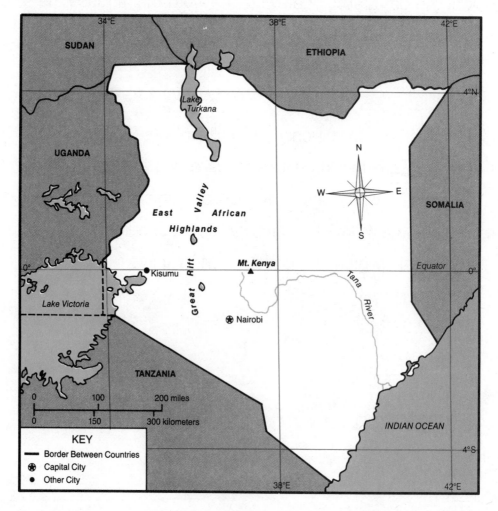

KEY
— Border Between Countries
⊛ Capital City
● Other City

Indian Ocean. The Equator goes through Kenya. Some parts of Kenya are very hot.

Kenya has many kinds of land. There are low coastal plains near the ocean. Away from the ocean are high plateaus. In most places, these areas get little rain. These dry plateaus cover three fourths of Kenya. Some of them are covered with savannas. Thousands of wild animals live there.

Lake Victoria is a huge lake in Africa. Part of this lake is on the west side of Kenya. The land around Lake Victoria gets a lot of rain. People do a lot of farming and fishing in this area.

Highlands make up the land in the southwest part of Kenya. Only one fifth of Kenya's land is in the highlands. But most of Kenya's people live in this area. Nairobi is Kenya's capital. It is one of Africa's largest cities. Nairobi is in Kenya's highlands. There is good soil for farming. There is a good climate.

Nairobi is the capital of Kenya.

The Great Rift Valley is in Kenya's highlands. The Rift is made of deep cracks in the earth. These cracks form valleys. The Great Rift is thousands of miles long. It goes through most of eastern Africa and into the Middle East.

Who are the people of Kenya? The people of Kenya are called Kenyans. Most Kenyans are black Africans. Kenya also has some Asians and whites. More white people live in Kenya than in any other country in eastern or western Africa.

Almost 20 million people live in Kenya. More than half of the people are Christians. Some people are Muslims. Many Kenyans follow traditional African religions.

The people of Kenya belong to 40 ethnic groups. The people speak many different languages. It has been hard for the many ethnic groups to get along with each other.

Like Nigeria, Kenya was ruled by Britain. Today Kenya is a free country. Kenyans wanted an African language to be their official language. Swahili is the country's official language.

Most Kenyans work at farming. The farmers live in villages. Many farmers do not use modern ways of farming. They try to grow enough food for their families. Many times they do not have enough crops to sell.

Not all farms in Kenya are small. There are large coffee and tea farms in the highlands. Coffee is an important cash crop. Kenya earns most of its money by exporting coffee to other countries.

Kenya also earns money from its tourist business. Every year thousands of people visit Kenya. The people come to see the many wild animals that live on the savannas. Kenya has large parks where people can see the wild animals.

Tourists visit Kenya to see the wild animals.

Kenya is not an industrial country. It is a developing country. Nigeria and most African countries are also developing countries. This means they are trying to start new businesses and factories. Many new factories have been built in Kenya. Today factories make chemicals, clothing, and paper. Kenya also has oil refineries. In refineries oil from other countries is cleaned and changed. Refined oil can be used by cars and factories.

Like other African countries, Kenya has many problems. Less than half of all Kenyans know how to read. The government is building schools. Kenya does not have enough farm land. Kenyans must learn to use irrigation to change dry land into farm land. Another problem is that Kenya's population is growing very fast. There are not enough jobs for all the people in Kenya. Kenyans are working on their problems. They are trying to build a better country.

Think, Remember, Write

A. Find the Answer

On your paper, copy the sentences that tell about Kenya. You should write 4 sentences.

1. Dry plateaus cover three fourths of Kenya.

2. The land near Lake Victoria is not good for farming.

3. Kenya's highlands have a good climate and good soil for farming.

4. Most of Kenya's people live in the highlands.

5. Kenya earns most of its money from exporting diamonds.

6. Kenya earns most of its money from exporting coffee.

B. Find the Meaning

Look up each word in a dictionary. Copy one meaning. Then write your own sentence about Kenya for that word.

1. coastal

2. valley

3. refinery

4. refine

C. Finish Up

Use the words in dark print to finish each sentence. Write the words you choose on your paper.

highlands	**Mombasa**	**coastal**	**Lake**	**Great**
Swahili	**refineries**	**Developing**	**Nairobi**	**fifth**

1. The _____ Rift Valley is made of deep cracks in the earth.

2. The capital of Kenya is _____.

3. _____ is Kenya's official language.

4. _____ Victoria is a huge lake in Africa.

5. Kenyans grow coffee on large farms in the _____.

6. Kenya has oil _____ to clean and change oil so that it can be used by cars and factories.

7. Only one _____ of Kenya's land is in the highlands.

8. Kenya has _____ plains near the ocean.

9. _____ countries are countries that are trying to start new businesses and factories.

10. _____ is a port city on the Indian Ocean.

Skill Words

line graphs   trends   period of time

Line graphs are used to show trends. Trends are changes that take place over a period of time.

The line graph on this page shows how Kenya's population has changed since 1970. A quick look at the graph tells you that the population has grown larger each year. Do you think Kenya's population next year will be larger than it is now?

KENYA'S POPULATION GROWTH SINCE 1970

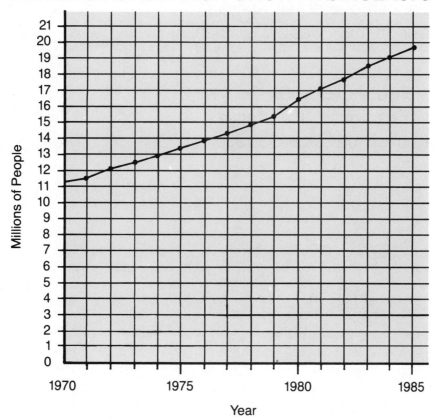

Year

A. Match Up

Look at the line graph on page 211. Then finish each sentence in Group A with an answer from Group B. Write the letter of the correct answer on your paper.

Group A	Group B

Group A

1. In 1970, Kenya's population was about ....

2. In 1975, Kenya's population was about ....

3. In 1980, Kenya's population was about ....

4. The graph does not show the year 1965. We can guess that Kenya's population in 1965 was .... than in 1970.

5. The graph does not show the year 1990. We can guess that Kenya's population will be .... in 1990.

Group B

a. smaller

b. larger

c. 16 million

d. 11 million

e. 13 million

CHAPTER 29

The Republic of South Africa

NEW WORDS: Dutch   Netherlands   Afrikaans   Coloreds
mixed races   apartheid   separate   protests   homelands

The Republic of South Africa is very different from other African countries. Half of the people live in cities. The country has good transportation. South Africa is not in the tropics. The summers are not very hot, and the winters are not very cold.

South Africa is near two oceans. The Atlantic Ocean is to the west. The Indian Ocean is to the east. The country has a long coast. There are four port cities on the coast. South Africa has a narrow coastal plain. Farms and beaches are there.

Much of the land in South Africa is plateaus. They are covered with grass. There are deserts in the northern and western parts of the country. The country has only a few rivers.

SOUTH AFRICA

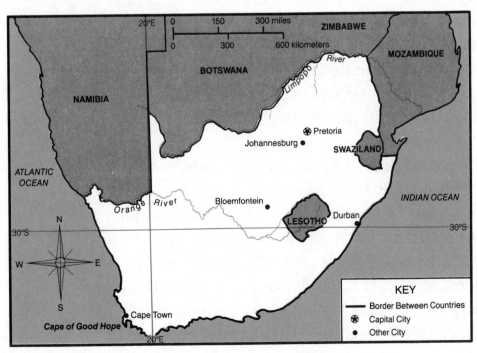

South Africa is very rich in natural resources. Most of the world's gold and diamonds come from South Africa. This country also has coal, iron, and other minerals. South Africa is not rich in oil. It must buy oil from other countries.

South Africa is the richest African country. It is an industrial country. There are more factories in South Africa than in any other African country. Mining is very important in South Africa. South Africans sell diamonds, gold, and metals to other countries. South Africa has modern farms. The country grows more food than it needs. South Africa exports food to other African countries.

The Dutch were the first white people to settle on South Africa's coast. They came from a country in Europe called the Netherlands. Many years later people from Britain came to South Africa. Blacks from other parts of Africa moved into South Africa. For a while Britain ruled all of South Africa. In 1910, South Africa became an independent country.

Today English and Afrikaans are the country's official languages. Afrikaans is a lot like the Dutch language. Blacks also speak their own ethnic languages.

Who are the people of South Africa today? There are 32 million people in this country. Most people are Christians. There are four big groups of people. Two thirds of the people in South Africa are blacks. One fifth of the people are whites. A small part of South Africa's people are Asians. Another group of South Africans is called Coloreds. Coloreds are people of mixed races. They may be of black and Asian descent. Other Coloreds are of white and black descent.

White people rule South Africa. They have made laws called apartheid laws. Apartheid laws keep the four groups of South Africans apart. Only white South Africans are allowed to vote. White South Africans make all the laws for the country. There are separate schools for each South African group. The best schools in South Africa are for white children.

Life is much harder for South Africans who are not white. Blacks, Coloreds, and Asians are poorer than white people.

They are paid less at their jobs. They are not allowed to do many kinds of work. Blacks are not allowed to live in the cities. They must live in special areas outside of the cities. There are not enough schools for black children. Half of South Africa's blacks do not know how to read and write.

This bench is for Coloreds and Asians only.

The apartheid laws are the biggest problem in South Africa today. The white people feel they built a modern country in South Africa. The whites do not want to lose their power. The blacks want a good life in South Africa too. They want the same rights that white people have. They want better jobs and schools. There have been large protests by groups of blacks in South Africa.

The government of South Africa has started to form homelands for black people. These lands are for ten important black ethnic groups. The homelands have less than one fourth of South Africa's land. White leaders want all blacks to move to them. Each one would become an independent black state. They would not be part of the Republic of South Africa.

South Africa is a beautiful, rich country. Perhaps one day all of its people will be able to have a good life in this country.

Black South Africans are building a home.

Think, Remember, Write

A. Locate the Answer

Write the correct answer to each question.

1. What ocean is to the east of South Africa?

   Atlantic   Indian   Pacific

2. What ocean is to the west of South Africa?

Atlantic   Indian   Pacific

3. How many people live in South Africa?

10 million   32 million   90 million

4. Which group of South Africans has the most people?

whites   blacks   Coloreds

5. Which group of South Africans can vote?

whites   blacks   Asians

6. What are the official languages of South Africa?

English and Swahili   French and Dutch   English and Afrikaans

B. True or False

Write **T** for each sentence that is true. Write **F** for each sentence that is false.

1. South Africa is a poor country.

2. There are many factories in South Africa.

3. South Africa exports food to other countries.

4. Tall mountains cover much of South Africa.

5. South Africa has few natural resources.

6. The Dutch came to South Africa from the Netherlands.

7. Apartheid laws keep the four groups of South Africans apart.

8. White leaders want all blacks to move to homelands.

C. Finish Up

Use the words in dark print to finish each sentence. Write the words you choose on your paper.

apartheid   **Britain**   **coastal**
oil   **diamonds**   **tropics**

1. South Africa is an African country that is not in the _____.

2. South Africa exports _____ and metals.

3. South Africa must buy _____ from other countries.

4. South Africa has farms and beaches on its _____ plain.

5. For a while _____ ruled all of South Africa.

6. The _____ laws are the biggest problem in South Africa today.

SKILL BUILDER 29: Understanding Pie Charts

Skill Words

pie chart   percent   multiply

A pie chart is a circle that has been divided into parts. Each part looks like a piece of pie. All the parts make up the whole circle.

The pie chart on page 219 shows how the people of South Africa are divided into four groups. The four groups make up the whole population of South Africa.

The pie chart shows us that only 3 percent (3%) of South Africans are Asians. There are 32 million people in South Africa. Multiply that number by 3 percent. Then you will know how many Asians live in South Africa.

A. Finish Up

Look at the pie chart again. Then use the words in dark print to finish each sentence. Write the words you choose on your paper.

blacks   **Asians**   **70%**   **17%**   **10%**   **3%**

1. The blacks are _____ of South Africa's population.

2. The whites are _____ of the population.

3. _____ of the people are Asians.

4. The Coloreds are _____ of the population.

5. _____ are the largest group.

6. _____ are the smallest group.

FOUR GROUPS OF SOUTH AFRICA'S PEOPLE

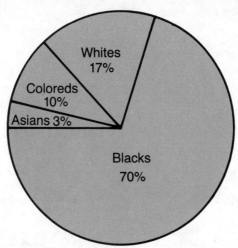

CHAPTER 30

Working for a Better Africa

NEW WORDS: corn   yield   college   poverty   malnutrition
sickness   medicine   insects   profits   Peace Corps

An African family is planting corn on its small farm.
The people work the same way Africans have worked for
hundreds of years. But this family will grow much more corn
than other Africans have grown. This family is planting new
kinds of corn seeds. These new seeds will yield much more
corn. Growing more food is one way people are working for a
better Africa.

What are some of the problems Africans face today?
Illiteracy is a very big problem in Africa. Most people do not
know how to read or write. Africans are building many new
schools. But less than one fifth of the children finish high
school. Few Africans go to college.

A classroom in Kenya

Poverty is another big problem. Most Africans are very poor. They earn less money in a year than many Americans earn in one week. Most African countries are too poor to build railroads, factories, and schools.

Malnutrition is also a problem. This means people do not eat enough of the right kinds of food. Many Africans are sick because they do not eat the right foods.

Sickness is another problem. Africa does not have enough hospitals and doctors. There is not enough medicine. In many places, the water is not safe for drinking. Many people get sick from using this water. There are dangerous insects that make Africans sick. These insects live in the rain forests. People get sick when they are bitten by these insects.

Poor ways of farming are another problem. Only a small part of Africa's land has good soil for farming. In many areas, there is not enough rain. Africans do not use good tools or fertilizer. They do not irrigate much of their dry land.

A small African village

How are Africans solving their many problems? Africans want to grow more food. People are trying to use more irrigation on the farms. Some Africans are learning how to use better seeds, tools, and fertilizers.

African governments are trying to start new industries. These will give people more jobs. New industries provide more money for people and for countries in Africa.

How does Africa get the money it needs to build factories? Sometimes government money is used to start new factories. Often people from Europe and the United States use their money to start businesses in Africa. The Americans and Europeans share their profits with African countries.

Many Americans are helping Africans solve some of their problems. These Americans are part of a group called the Peace Corps. Peace Corps members work for two years in developing countries. In Africa, they help some people

The Peace Corps has helped Africans learn new skills.

become teachers. They start schools. They teach Africans better ways to grow food. They help Africans learn how to stay healthy. People from other countries are also working in Africa. They are doing the same kinds of jobs that Peace Corps members do. They are all teaching Africans how to help themselves.

Africa's people are working to solve their problems. Countries are starting new industries. People are growing more food. Each year more children go to school. People are learning about better health care. They are trying to destroy dangerous insects. Africa is slowly becoming a better place to live.

Think, Remember, Write

A. True or False

Write **T** for each sentence that is true. Write **F** for each sentence that is false.

1. Most people in Africa do not know how to read or write.

2. Most Africans earn more money than Americans.

3. Some Africans are planting new kinds of seeds that yield more crops.

4. Poverty and sickness are problems in Africa.

5. There are too many doctors and hospitals in Africa.

6. Africa does not need more industries.

7. Peace Corps members are teaching Africans better ways to grow food.

8. The United States is the only country that is helping Africa.

B. Finish Up

Use the words in dark print to finish each sentence. Write the words you choose on your paper.

insects   industries   Peace Corps
yield   Malnutrition

1. People are planting new kinds of corn seeds that will _____ more corn.

2. _____ means people are sick because they do not eat enough of the right kinds of foods.

3. Many Africans get sick because they are bitten by dangerous _____.

4. New _____ provide more money for people and for countries in Africa.

5. _____ members work for two years in developing countries.

C. Find the Answer

On your paper, copy the sentences that tell how people are working for a better Africa. You should write 6 sentences.

1. Africans are building many new schools.

2. Every African is studying at a college.

3. All African farmers are working the same way farmers worked long ago.

4. Africans are learning how to use better seeds, tools, and fertilizers.

5. Africans are trying to use more irrigation on the farms.

6. Americans and Europeans are using their money to start new businesses in African countries.

7. African governments are using their money to start new factories.

8. All Africans are becoming factory workers.

9. People in the Peace Corps are teaching Africans how to help themselves.

SKILL BUILDER 30: Understanding Tables

A table lists groups of facts. Tables are used to learn facts quickly. It is easy to compare facts in a table. Read the table below to learn facts about Kenya, Nigeria, and South Africa.

THREE AFRICAN COUNTRIES THAT ARE SOUTH OF THE SAHARA

Country	Population	Natural Resources	Important Exports	Official Language
Nigeria	90 million	oil, coal iron, tin	oil, cocoa, palm oil	English
Kenya	20 million	trees, wild animals, good soil in the highlands	coffee, tea, refined oil	Swahili
South Africa	32 million	gold, diamonds, coal, iron, tin	diamonds, gold, metals, food	English, Afrikaans

A. Write the Answer

Look at the table again. Write a sentence to answer each question.

1. What are Kenya's natural resources?

2. What is Kenya's population?

3. What does Nigeria export?

4. What is Nigeria's official language?

5. What are South Africa's natural resources?

6. What does South Africa export?

7. Which country has two official languages?

8. Which country has the largest population?

UNIT SEVEN

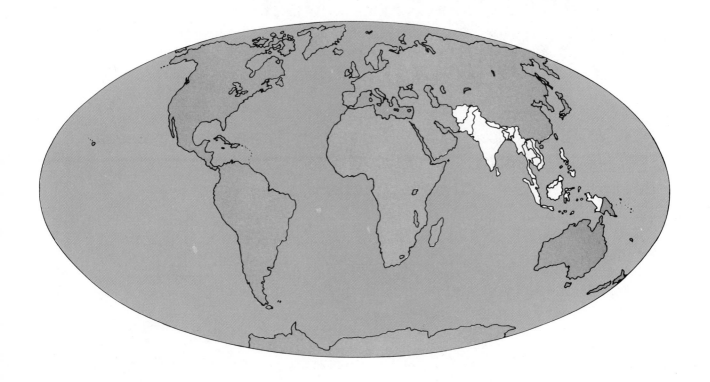

South and Southeast Asia

You will read these chapters in Unit 7:

227

CHAPTER 31

Getting to Know South and Southeast Asia

NEW WORDS: rice   India   Pakistan   Bangladesh   Indonesia
Philippines   monsoon   seasonal   Himalaya Mountains
Buddhists   Hindus   Thailand   rubber   spices   tin

Would you like to eat rice every day? You would be
eating lots of rice if you lived in South and Southeast Asia.
Rice would be your most important food.

Harvesting rice in Indonesia

The land of South and Southeast Asia is between two oceans. This area is between the Indian and Pacific oceans. This area has two parts. South Asia is one part. India, Pakistan, and Bangladesh are in South Asia. Southeast Asia is the other part of this area. Southeast Asia has a long coast. Most places are near the sea. Southeast Asia has many small countries. It also has two large countries. Indonesia and the Philippines are the largest countries. They are made of large groups of islands.

This fishing village is in the country of Malaysia.

Most countries in South and Southeast Asia are in the tropics. Most countries of the area get monsoon winds. These are seasonal winds. From April until October, monsoon winds blow in one direction. Then they blow in a different direction for the rest of the year.

How do the monsoon winds help this area? They are important because they bring rain to this area. The people of this area need these rains to grow food.

There are many kinds of land in this area. The tall Himalaya Mountains separate South Asia from the rest of Asia. Many countries have mountains. There are plains and plateaus. There are long rivers. Many places in Southeast Asia have rain forests.

The Himalayas are the world's highest mountains.

The population of South and Southeast Asia is very large. One fourth of all the people in the world live in this area. The number of people is growing very fast.

The people of this area speak many different languages. They come from many ethnic groups. They belong to four religious groups. Most people in Southeast Asia are Buddhists. In India, most people are Hindus. In Indonesia, Bangladesh, and Pakistan, most people are Muslims. Most people in the Philippines are Christians.

230

Most countries have good soil for farming. But most farms are small. The people grow rice on these small farms.

For hundreds of years, most of this area was ruled by Britain, France, and the Netherlands. Only Thailand remained free. Now all the countries of the area are free.

The Europeans sent natural resources from the Asian countries to Europe. The Europeans also started some large farms. Cash crops are grown on these large farms. Today these cash crops are sold to many countries. Rubber, tea, sugar, coffee, and spices are some cash crops of this area.

South and Southeast Asia have important natural resources. Indonesia is rich in oil. A few countries are rich in tin. South Asia has coal and iron. Some countries sell their resources to earn money. But most countries have not started many industries. The countries of South and Southeast Asia are still developing countries.

India is the largest country in this area. In the next chapters, you will learn about life in India.

Think, Remember, Write

A. Write the Answer

Write a sentence to answer each question.

1. What is the most important food in South and Southeast Asia?

2. What are four cash crops in this area?

3. What are four natural resources?

4. Which is the largest country in the area?

B. Finish Up

Use the words in dark print to finish each sentence. Write the words you choose on your paper.

monsoon   **tropics**   **Himalaya**   **Buddhist**

1. Most countries in South and Southeast Asia are in the _____.

2. The _____ winds bring heavy rain to most countries in South and Southeast Asia.

3. The _____ Mountains separate South Asia from the rest of Asia.

4. People follow Christian, Muslim, Hindu, and _____ religions in South and Southeast Asia.

C. Map Study

Look at the map of South and Southeast Asia on page 233. Then use facts from the map to answer each question in Group A with an item from Group B. Write the letter of the correct answer on your paper.

Group A

1. What country is west of India?

2. What country is east of India?

3. What two countries in Southeast Asia are made of groups of islands?

4. What big country is north of Southeast Asia?

Group B

a. Indonesia and the Philippines

b. China

c. Pakistan

d. Bangladesh

SOUTH AND SOUTHEAST ASIA

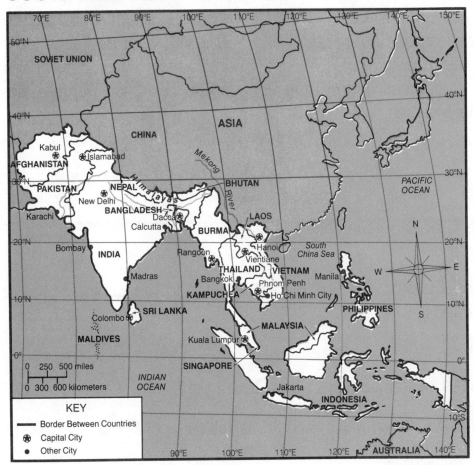

SKILL BUILDER 31: Reviewing Latitude and Longitude

Skill Words

latitude	imaginary	longitude
degrees	Prime Meridian	Madras

Lines of latitude are imaginary lines. They run east and west around the earth. Lines of longitude are imaginary lines too. They run north and south around the earth. Lines of longitude meet at the North and South poles.

Latitude and longitude are measured in degrees. The Equator is the line of latitude that goes around the center of the earth. It is 0° latitude. The most important line of longitude is the Prime Meridian. The Prime Meridian is at 0° longitude.

Lines of latitude and longitude form grids on maps. These grids help us find places on the maps. We can use lines of latitude and longitude to find places on a map of South and Southeast Asia. Madras is a city in India. It has a latitude of 13°N and a longitude of 80°E. This means Madras is 13 degrees north of the Equator. Madras is 80 degrees east of the Prime Meridian.

A. True or False

Write **T** for each sentence that is true. Write **F** for each sentence that is false.

1. The Equator is a line of latitude around the center of the earth.

2. Lines of latitude are measured in inches.

3. Lines of longitude run east and west.

4. The Prime Meridian is at 0° longitude.

B. Match Up

Look at the map of South and Southeast Asia on page 233. Then finish each sentence in Group A with an answer from Group B. Write the letter of the correct answer on your paper.

Group A	Group B
1. The Equator goes through the country of	a. 1°N, 104°E
2. Singapore is close to the Equator. Its latitude and longitude are	b. 6°S, 106°E
3. Jakarta is south of the Equator. Its latitude and longitude are	c. New Delhi
4. The city of .... has a latitude and longitude of 28°N, 77°E.	d. Indonesia

CHAPTER 32

India: A Country of Villages

NEW WORDS: seasons   Indus River   Ganges River
Brahmaputra River   fertile plain   Deccan Plateau   Indians
Hindi   paved roads   Calcutta   New Delhi   system

Everywhere in India, people are happy. They have
waited many months for the summer monsoons to bring rain.

INDIA

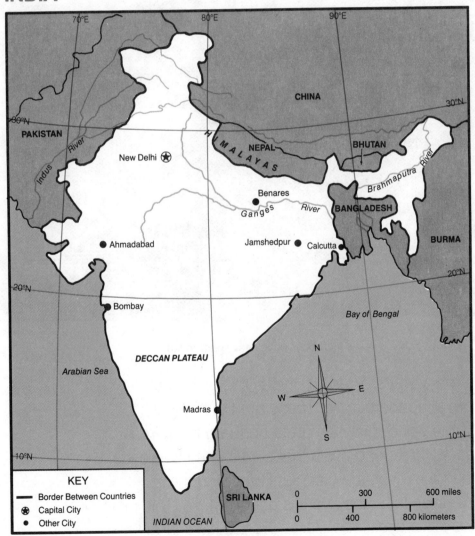

KEY
— Border Between Countries
✪ Capital City
● Other City

Now it is June, and the rains have started. The rains are very important to India. Without them people cannot grow food.

India is a big country. More than 730 million people live in India. It is one third the size of the United States. But India has three times as many people as the United States. It has the second largest population in the world.

India has three seasons. In one season the weather is cool and dry. In another season the weather is very hot and dry. The rains come during the hot, wet season. It is hot and rainy from June to September.

The monsoons bring heavy rains to India.

There are many kinds of land in India. The tall Himalaya Mountains are in northern India. These are the highest mountains in the world. They separate northern India from China. India has three long rivers that start in the Himalayas. They are the Indus River, the Ganges River, and the Brahmaputra River. Near the rivers is a fertile plain. This plain is south of the Himalayas. The plain covers a lot of land in

These Hindus are bathing in the Ganges River.

Pakistan, India, and Bangladesh. It is very crowded. Most of India's food is grown on this plain.

The Deccan Plateau is south of the fertile plain. The Deccan Plateau gets little rain. The land is not good farm land. Many of India's natural resources are found in the Deccan Plateau.

Southern India is a large V-shaped peninsula. It has water on two sides. India has coastal plains near the sea. These plains get a lot of rain. They have good farm land.

The people of India are called Indians. There are 16 languages that are spoken in India. It is hard for people from different parts of India to understand each other. Hindi and English are India's official languages.

Most Indians live in small villages. There are thousands of villages in the country. Most villages do not have electricity. They do not have paved roads. Village homes do not have running water. Most village people are poor farmers.

Most Indians live in small villages.

Not all of India's people live in villages. One fourth of the people live in cities. Calcutta is India's largest city. More than ten million people live in this city. New Delhi is India's capital. Many poor farmers have left their villages and moved to the cities. The cities have become very crowded.

India has the largest railroad system in Asia. Large cities have good transportation. It is easy to go between large cities. But it is very hard to get to the thousands of small villages. There are few roads that join the villages to other parts of the country.

The government of India is a democracy. For many years, Britain ruled India. Now India is a free country. People vote for their government leaders. The country has its Parliament. The country's leader is the prime minister.

India is a country with many natural resources. India has lots of coal and iron. It has natural gas. It has some gold, silver, and diamonds. There are other metals too. India has lots of water power. But there is little oil.

India is a developing country. The country is trying to start new industries. About five million Indians now work in factories. But this is only a very small part of India's huge population. India's factories make steel. They make cotton cloth.

India does not use many of its natural resources. It is a poor country with big problems. What are they? How are people trying to solve them? The answers are in the next chapter.

Think, Remember, Write

A. Match Up

Finish each sentence in Group A with an answer from Group B. Write the letter of the correct answer on your paper.

Group A	Group B
1. Southern India is a large	a. democracy
2. The two official languages of India are	b. peninsula
	c. English and Hindi
3. India's capital city is	d. New Delhi
4. The government of India is a	e. villages
5. There are few roads that join .... to other parts of India.	

B. Finish the Sentence

Write the word that finishes the sentence.

1. India has ≡ million people.

   60   130   730

2. India gets monsoon rains during the ≡ season.

   cool, dry   hot, wet   hot, dry

3. The ≡ Mountains are in northern India.

   Kilimanjaro   Himalaya   Andes

4. Three important Indian rivers are the Indus, Ganges, and ≡.

   Brahmaputra   Nile   Tigris

5. Most Indians live on the ≡.

   Himalaya Mountains   Deccan Plateau   fertile plain

6. Most of India's natural resources are in the ≡.

   Himalaya Mountains   Deccan Plateau   fertile plain

7. The largest city in India is ≡.

   Calcutta   New Delhi   Nairobi

8. The leader of India is the ≡.

   prime minister   president   queen

C. Write It Right

The words in the sentences below are mixed up. Write each sentence correctly.

1. Deccan Plateau The good farm land. have not does

2. spoken languages that are 16 in India. There are

3. of people India's One fourth in cities. live

4. in Asia. largest railroad system India the has

5. do not Most villages have water. running or paved roads

SKILL BUILDER 32: Reviewing Relief Maps

Skill Words

relief maps

You learned that relief maps help you find out about the kinds of land a country has. Relief maps show where there are plains and plateaus. They show mountains and highlands. The relief map of India on this page shows the different kinds of land in that country.

RELIEF MAP OF INDIA

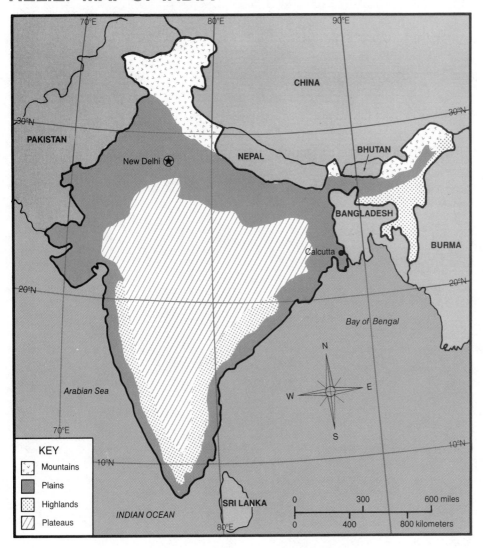

A. True or False

Look at the relief map of India on page 241. Then write **T** for each sentence that is true. Write **F** for each sentence that is false.

1. India has tall mountains in the northeast.

2. India has tall mountains in the southeast.

3. There are tall mountains on the west coast.

4. There are tall mountains near China.

5. New Delhi and Calcutta are in the plains.

6. There are plains near Pakistan.

7. Northern India has a plateau.

8. Central India has a plateau.

9. There are highlands in the south.

10. There are highlands in the north.

CHAPTER 33

India: A Crowded Land

NEW WORDS: sacred   caste system   caste   priests
Green Revolution   miracle seeds   grain   store   surplus

It is a hot night in Calcutta. Many poor people are
sleeping on the city streets. Many cows are in the streets too.
The cows walk wherever they wish. Why are there so many
poor Indians? Why are there so many cows on city streets?
The answers are in this chapter.

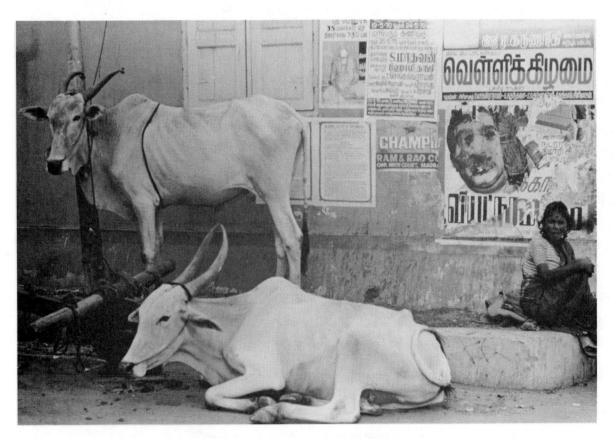

Hindus believe that cows are sacred animals.

Religion is very important to the people of India. Most
Indians believe in the Hindu religion. The country also has

millions of Muslims. There are Christians in many parts of India.

Hindus believe that people should not hurt animals. They believe that cows are sacred animals. Hindus drink milk from cows. They use cows to help them do farm work. But they do not eat meat from cows.

The caste system is part of the Hindu religion. A caste is a group of people. Every Hindu is born into a caste. Hindu priests and their families are in the highest group. Farmers are in a lower group. There are more than 3,000 castes. People cannot change their caste. People must marry another person from their group.

Many people believe that the caste system keeps India poor. People cannot get better jobs by studying and working hard. It is hard for people to make their lives better.

The government of India is working to end the caste system. It is now easier for people in lower groups to get better jobs. But it will take many years before Hindus end their caste system.

Religion has caused fighting in India. There have often been fights between Hindus and Muslims. There have been fights between Hindus and people of other religious groups too. Many people have died during these fights.

Illiteracy is another problem in India. Almost two thirds of the people cannot read or write. Only half of India's children go to school.

Overpopulation is another reason India is a poor country. India is very crowded. The number of people is growing very fast. Most families are proud when they have many children. The Indian government is trying to teach families to have fewer children.

Most Indians earn their living by farming. For many years, the leaders thought that India would solve its many problems by becoming an industrial country. But this did not work. Today the leaders believe better ways to farm will solve many problems. The government wants people to learn to be better farmers.

India has the second largest population in the world.

Today some parts of India are having a Green Revolution. A Green Revolution means people are learning new ways to grow much more food. In many places, Indian farmers are using miracle seeds. These seeds grow much faster. They yield better crops. In the past, farmers grew one crop each year. With miracle seeds, farmers can grow three crops in a year. Farmers are learning to use fertilizers to grow more food. They are learning to irrigate their land.

The Green Revolution has already helped India. For many years, India had to import grain. Rice and wheat are two kinds of grain. Now India is able to export grain. India is able to store some of its rice and wheat. Indians use this grain in years when the monsoons do not bring enough rain.

But India is still a very poor country. Most farmers have few modern tools. They use animals to do the work that machines

Animals are used for many jobs on Indian farms.

would do faster and better. Indian farmers need better tools, machines, and irrigation.

India needs many more roads. It is hard for village farmers to sell their surplus, or extra, crops. They do not have the transportation to send their surplus crops to other villages and cities.

Indians are slowly solving their problems. They are building more schools. They are using better ways of farming. But Indians have a lot more work to do. Indians must use their natural resources. They need more factories and better transportation.

Think, Remember, Write

A. True or False

Write **T** for each sentence that is true. Write **F** for each sentence that is false.

1. Most Indians are Muslims.

2. People must marry a person from their own caste.

3. There have never been fights between people of different religions in India.

4. All children in India go to school.

5. The Green Revolution is helping people grow more crops with miracle seeds.

B. Finish Up

Use the words in dark print to finish each sentence. Write the words you choose on your paper.

farming   animals   caste
priests   miracle

1. Many people believe that the _____ system keeps India poor.

2. Hindu _____ are in the highest caste.

3. Most Indians earn their living by _____.

4. Farmers are using _____ seeds to grow more crops.

5. Most Indian farmers use _____ instead of machines to do the farm work.

C. Finish the Sentence

Write the word that finishes the sentence.

1. Every Hindu is born into a group called a ══ .

   caste   school   herd

2. Hindus believe ══ are sacred animals.

   birds   dogs   cows

3. ══ seeds grow faster and yield more food.

   Corn   Miracle   Brown

4. ══ is a big problem in India.

   Illiteracy   Language   Vacation

5. The Green ══ is helping Indians use new ways to grow more food.

   Religion   Revolution   Restaurant

6. Sometimes Indian farmers have a ══ of grain.

   surplus   city   village

7. The government is trying to teach families to have fewer ══ .

   crops   children   tools

8. Indians ══ rice and wheat so they will have food when there is little rain.

   waste   store   burn

9. Rice and wheat are two kinds of ══ .

   milk   meat   grain

10. Most Indians believe in the ══ religion.

    Jewish   Hindu   Christian

Skill Words

distance scales   Benares   Jamshedpur

Distance scales help us find distances between places on maps. On the map on this page, one inch is the same as 400 miles in India. Two inches would be 800 miles. How many miles would 3 inches be? How many miles would ½ inch be? There is ½ inch between the cities of Calcutta and Jamshedpur. In India, these cities are about 200 miles apart.

INDIA

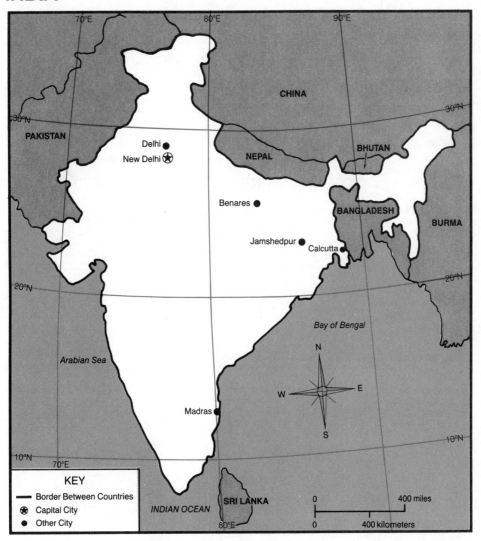

A. Locate the Answer

Look at the map of India on page 249. Then write the correct answer to each question.

1. How many inches are between the north and south of India?

    1   2   5

2. What is the distance between the north and south of India?

    300 miles   600 miles   2,000 miles

3. How many inches are between Delhi and Calcutta?

    1   2   3½

4. What is the distance between Delhi and Calcutta?

    100 miles   800 miles   1,200 miles

B. Write the Answer

Write a sentence to answer each question.

1. Which city is farthest from Delhi, Benares or Calcutta?

2. Which city is closest to Madras, Calcutta or Delhi?

CHAPTER 34

Understanding the Problems of South and Southeast Asia

NEW WORDS: Singapore Vietnam non-Communists
Indochina Peninsula Laos Kampuchea destroyed
unstable enemy

Many people around the world enjoy drinking tea. Most of the tea comes from the countries of South and Southeast Asia.

Most of the world's tea comes from South and Southeast Asia.

All the countries of South and Southeast Asia are developing countries. These countries share some of the problems that are found in Latin America, the Middle East, and Africa. There is not enough good transportation. There is too much poverty. The number of people is growing very fast.

There is a lot of illiteracy in this part of the world. Only one third of the people in this area know how to read and write. Some countries have been working very hard to solve this problem. At one time most people in Indonesia were illiterate. Today two thirds of the people can read. In the Philippines, Singapore, Thailand, and Vietnam, three fourths of the people have learned to read and write.

More and more people in Southeast Asia have learned to read and write.

There is not much oil in the countries of this area. Only Indonesia has some oil. Modern countries need oil for their farm machines. They need oil for factories and cars. Many countries must import their oil. It is hard for poor countries to pay for the oil they need.

Most farmers in South and Southeast Asia do not use modern ways of farming. In modern countries, machines do most of the farm work. In this area, people and animals do the farm work. Better machines and good tools would help farmers do a better job.

Do you remember that India is having a Green Revolution? India is now able to grow more food. Today many countries in South and Southeast Asia are having a Green Revolution. Farmers in many places are using miracle seeds and fertilizers. Now many farmers are able to grow three or four crops each year. There is more food for the area's many people.

The Green Revolution has not come to every part of South and Southeast Asia. Many places still need miracle seeds. Most farmers still need better farm machines and tools.

New kinds of seeds and fertilizers help farmers.

War is one of the biggest problems in South and Southeast Asia. Sometimes Hindus and Muslims fight against each other. Today many countries in Southeast Asia have Communist governments. Communists would like to rule all of Southeast Asia. There has been fighting between Communists and non-Communists. Non-Communists are people who are against communism.

Many wars have been fought on the Indochina Peninsula. This is part of Southeast Asia. Thailand, Laos, Vietnam, and Kampuchea are the four countries of Indochina. For almost 30 years, there was fighting in the country of Vietnam. Today Communists rule all of Vietnam. Communists have fought in Kampuchea. They fought in Laos. They now rule these countries. Only Thailand has remained non-Communist.

Southeast Asia has been hurt by many years of war. Villages and farms have been destroyed. Thousands of people have been killed. Money that is needed to build factories and schools has been spent on wars. Peace has still not come to this area.

Many governments in South and Southeast Asia are unstable. Unstable governments are not strong. They do not rule well. Often government leaders have been attacked and killed by enemy groups. Then the enemy groups try to form new governments. Often the new governments are also unstable. The countries of this area need strong governments. They need good leaders to help them solve their problems.

Each year the population of South and Southeast Asia grows larger. Each year the people try to grow more food. The Green Revolution is helping the people of this area. The people need peace and strong governments. With peace, people can work together for a better life in this crowded part of the world.

Think, Remember, Write

A. Find the Answer

On your paper, copy each sentence that tells about the problems of South and Southeast Asia. You should write 4 sentences.

1. Many people are illiterate.

2. Many countries do not grow enough food.

3. There are too many big farm machines.

4. Some countries have too much oil.

5. Communists have caused a lot of fighting in Southeast Asia.

6. Many governments are unstable.

B. Match Up

Finish each sentence in Group A with an answer from Group B. Write the letter of the correct answer on your paper.

Group A	Group B
1. The number of people in South and Southeast Asia is _____.	a. Communist governments
2. People who live in small villages do not have _____.	b. enemy groups
3. _____ are people who are against communism.	c. non-Communists
4. Vietnam, Kampuchea, and Laos have _____.	d. growing very fast
5. Many government leaders have been killed by _____.	e. good transportation

C. Write It Right

The words in the sentences below are mixed up. Write each sentence correctly.

1. South and Southeast Asia. countries the of Most of comes from the tea

2. can read of the people Three fourths and Singapore, Thailand, Vietnam. in the Philippines,

3. Revolution Green The crops each year. three or four grow is farmers helping

4. rule all Communists Southeast Asia. would like to of

5. Indochina Peninsula. four countries are the of the Vietnam, Kampuchea, Laos, and Thailand

SKILL BUILDER 34: Reviewing Tables

Skill Words

fact tables	Jakarta	Islamabad	Manila
Bangkok	textiles	coconut	

Fact tables help us learn facts quickly. The table on page 257 helps us learn facts about five countries in South and Southeast Asia. Read the facts about each country. Then answer the questions.

A. Write the Answer

Write a sentence to answer each question.

1. Which country has a large Buddhist population?

2. What does the Philippines export?

3. What is the capital of Pakistan?

4. Where is Jakarta?

5. Which country has the smallest population?

6. Which country has the largest population?

FIVE COUNTRIES OF SOUTH AND SOUTHEAST ASIA

Country	Population	Capital	Major Religion	Exports
India	730 million	New Delhi	Hindu	textiles, clothing, tea
Indonesia	170 million	Jakarta	Islam	oil, natural gas
Pakistan	91 million	Islamabad	Islam	cotton, rice, carpets
Philippines	55 million	Manila	Catholic	coconut goods, sugar, lumber
Thailand	50 million	Bangkok	Buddhist	rice, rubber, tin

UNIT EIGHT

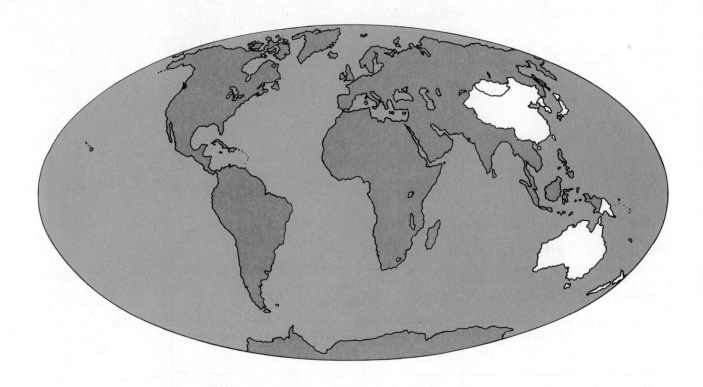

East Asia and the Pacific

You will read these chapters in Unit 8:

CHAPTER 35

East Asia and the Pacific

NEW WORDS: bicycle camera Australia Taiwan Japan China Hong Kong North Korea South Korea Oceania New Zealand earthquakes volcanoes erupt lava

An American mother went shopping for her family. She bought a wool coat for her son. She bought a bicycle for her daughter. She bought a camera for her husband. She bought

EAST ASIA AND THE PACIFIC

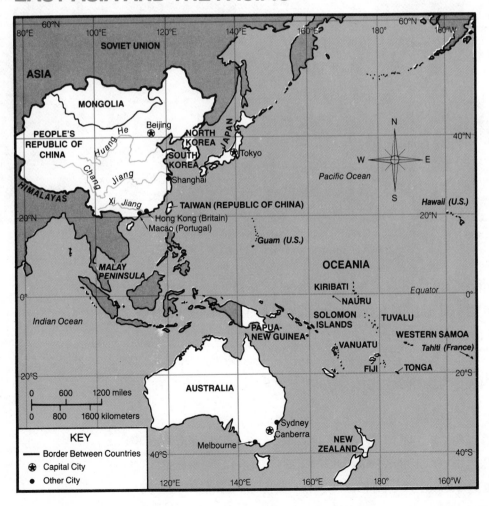

everything in an American store. But all these things were made in East Asia and the Pacific. The wool came from Australia. The bicycle came from Taiwan. The camera was made in Japan. American stores sell many goods from these far-off lands.

One fourth of the world's people live in East Asia and the Pacific. Most of the people of the area live in East Asia. Which countries are in East Asia? China, Japan, and Hong Kong are in East Asia. North Korea, South Korea, and Taiwan are also in East Asia. All of these countries are very crowded. China is the largest country in East Asia. China has more people than any other country in the world.

Japan is one of the crowded lands of East Asia.

The Pacific Ocean is huge. It is the largest ocean. There are thousands of islands in the Pacific Ocean. The islands of the Pacific are called Oceania. The continent of Australia is part of Oceania. New Zealand is also in Oceania. The lands of Oceania are not crowded. There is room for many more people.

There are many kinds of land in East Asia and the Pacific. Some areas have plains and plateaus. There are deserts in Australia and western China. Large parts of East Asia are covered with mountains. Many islands in the Pacific are also covered with mountains.

This part of the world has many earthquakes. The ground shakes, and sometimes the land cracks. Many people can be killed during a bad earthquake. Buildings are destroyed. There have been earthquakes in Japan and China. Some Pacific islands have had them too.

Volcanoes are also found in this area. Some are in Japan. Some are in Oceania. A volcano is a mountain that is open at the top. Sometimes it can erupt. Gases and hot lava, or melted rock, pour out. This covers the land around the volcano. People who are near are killed. These volcanoes are very dangerous. There are more volcanoes and earthquakes in this area than in any other part of the world.

There are many different climates in East Asia and the Pacific. The monsoons bring summer rains to the coasts of East Asia. Most of East Asia has cold, dry winters. Areas that are far from the Pacific get little rain during the year. Many places in China and Australia do not get enough rain.

The best climates in this area are between the 20° and 50° latitudes. In Australia and New Zealand, this is south of the Equator. In East Asia, it is north of the Equator. Most people of the area live between these latitudes.

This house is on the island of Tonga.

Different kinds of governments can be found in this area. Australia and Japan are democracies. So is New Zealand. China and North Korea are ruled by Communists. Some countries have dictators. A few islands are ruled by other countries.

The people of this area earn money in many different ways. Japan, Taiwan, and Australia are industrial countries. Most people in the small countries of Oceania earn their living by fishing and farming. China is a developing country. Most people in China are farmers. But many people now work in factories.

You will read about three important countries of this area in this unit. You will learn about China, Japan, and Australia. You will learn how people live in these far-off lands.

Think, Remember, Write

A. Write It Right

The words in the sentences below are mixed up. Write each sentence correctly.

1. East Pacific Asia and the Many parts with mountains. of covered are

2. in Australia and China. are There deserts

3. gets summer rains the Asia East near coast.

4. been earthquakes in Japan China. and There have

5. in Volcanoes found Japan Oceania. and are

B. Finish Up

Use the words in dark print to finish each sentence. Write the words you choose on your paper.

earthquake   **fourth**   **Taiwan**   **erupts**

volcano   **New Zealand**

1. North Korea, South Korea, Hong Kong, and _____ are some of the countries in East Asia.

2. Australia and _____ are large countries in Oceania.

3. One _____ of the world's people live in East Asia and the Pacific.

4. During an _____, the ground shakes and cracks.

5. A _____ is a mountain that is open at the top.

6. When a volcano _____, gases and hot lava pour out of the top.

C. Write the Answer

Write a sentence to answer each question.

1. What is the largest country in East Asia?

2. What are the island countries of the Pacific called?

3. What country in Oceania is a continent?

4. Between which latitudes do most people live?

5. Which countries are democracies?

6. Which countries are ruled by Communists?

Skill Words

picture graphs   telephone   assume

Picture graphs use symbols to show numbers of things. Picture graphs help you learn facts quickly.

The picture graph shows how many telephones are used in four countries of East Asia and the Pacific. Telephone symbols are used on this graph. Each symbol stands for one million telephones.

China has the largest population in this area. From the graph, we see that China has a little more than two million telephones. China has fewer telephones than Australia, Japan, and Taiwan. We can assume that most people in China do not own telephones.

TELEPHONES IN USE

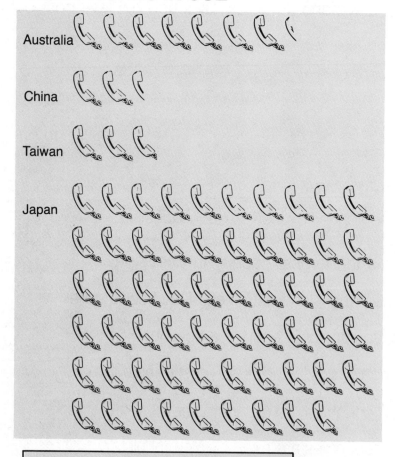

= 1,000,000 telephones

A. Finish the Sentence

Look at the picture graph. Then write the word that finishes the sentence.

1. Taiwan has almost ═══ million telephones.

   two   three   seven

2. Australia has a little more than ═══ million telephones.

   two   three   seven

3. Japan has ═══ million telephones.

   10   20   59

4. The country with the most telephones is ═══.

   Japan   Australia   Taiwan

5. Taiwan has fewer people but more telephones than ═══.

   China   Australia   Japan

CHAPTER 36

China: A Very Old Country

NEW WORDS: Beijing private billion Chinese emperors
Huang He Chang Jiang Xi Jiang soybeans

Beijing is China's capital city. There are people everywhere. There are also many bicycles. There are no private cars on the streets of Beijing. People do not have their own cars in China. Most people use bicycles.

CHINA

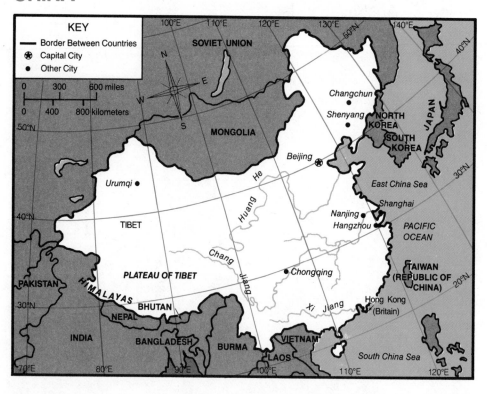

China is a huge country. It is the third largest country in the world. More than one billion people live in China. It has one fifth of the world's people.

Many people in Beijing use bicycles.

The people of China are called Chinese. Most people speak the Chinese language. They write their language with many symbols. There is one for each word.

China is a very old country. For hundreds of years, China was led by rulers called emperors. Most Chinese were poor. They did not know how to read.

China changed after World War II. Many people became Communists. The Communists wanted to rule all of China. There were many non-Communists too. These groups fought against each other. In 1949, the Communists won the war. China became a Communist country. The non-Communists moved to the island of Taiwan. Today there is a non-Communist Chinese country on Taiwan.

Most Chinese live better than they did before the Communists ruled. The people are poor, but they have enough food. All children go to school. Most people have learned how to read.

The Communists brought other changes to China. Religion is no longer important in China. Children are taught to care more about their country than about their families.

There is little freedom in China today. The government decides what should be said in newspapers, books, and movies. The government runs all the farms and factories. There are secret police in China. The secret police look for people who might be against the government.

China is ruled by a Communist party. The party makes all of China's laws. Only a few people can belong to the party. The leader of the party rules China. China's leader has a lot of power.

China is a big country with many kinds of land. Mountains cover one third of China. There is a large desert in the west. Eastern China has a long coast. The China Sea is to the east of the country. Most people live in eastern China. Most of China's farm land is in this part of the country.

China has three big rivers. One is the Huang He (Yellow River). The others are the Chang Jiang (Yangtze River) and the Xi Jiang (West River). Most of China's farm land is between these rivers. People sail on the Xi Jiang and the Chang Jiang. Large ships can sail on these rivers. The Chang Jiang is the longest river in China.

Floods have always been a problem on the Huang He. For thousands of years, the floods of the Huang He have destroyed farms and towns. Today the Chinese work hard to stop the Huang He from flooding the land.

China has many climates. The monsoons bring rain to eastern China in the summer. There is less rain in the winter. The southeast is warmer and wetter than other parts of the country. The Chinese grow rice there. Northwestern China is very dry. Summers are hot. Winters are very cold. There is little farming there. Many people in this area raise sheep. China's northeast is good for farming. The weather is cooler than in the south. Rice cannot grow in the north. Wheat, corn, and soybeans are grown there.

Rice is grown in the warm, wet southeast of China.

China is only a little larger than the United States. But China has five times more people than the United States. China also has much less farm land. What is it like to live in this huge Communist land? The answer is in the next chapter.

Think, Remember, Write

A. Finish the Sentence

Write the word that finishes the sentence.

1. China has more than one ▬▬ people.

   thousand   million   billion

2. ▬▬ cover one third of China.

   Lakes   Mountains   Volcanoes

3. People sail on the Chang Jiang and on the ▬▬.

   Xi Jiang   Huang He   Ganges River

4. The Chinese grow rice in the warm ▬▬.

   southeast   northwest   northeast

5. People raise sheep in the dry ═══.

   southeast   northwest   northeast

B. Match Up

Finish each sentence in Group A with an answer from Group B. Write the letter of the correct answer on your paper.

<u>Group A</u>

1. The capital of China is _____.

2. There is a non-Communist Chinese country on the island of _____.

3. There have been floods on the _____.

4. The longest river in China is the _____.

5. Most people live in _____.

<u>Group B</u>

a. Chang Jiang

b. Beijing

c. Huang He

d. Taiwan

e. eastern China

C. True or False

Write **T** for each sentence that is true. Write **F** for each sentence that is false.

1. China became a Communist country in 1980.

2. The leader of the Communist party rules China.

3. The Communists have taught children to care more about their country than about their families.

4. Today the Chinese have enough to eat.

5. Most Chinese have learned how to read.

6. Most Chinese live in western China.

Skill Words

climate maps   taiga   continental
moist   subtropical

We use climate maps to learn about the different kinds of weather in an area. China is a large country with many climates. The map on this page shows six climates that are found in China.

A taiga climate has long, cold, snowy winters and short, warm summers. A continental climate has cold, dry winters and hot, moist summers. A subtropical monsoon climate has cool, dry winters and hot, wet summers. A desert climate has hot summers, mild winters, and almost no rain. A steppes climate has a hot, dry season for nine months and cold winters with a little rain. A mountain and highland climate has rain or snow in the winters and dry summers.

CLIMATE MAP OF CHINA

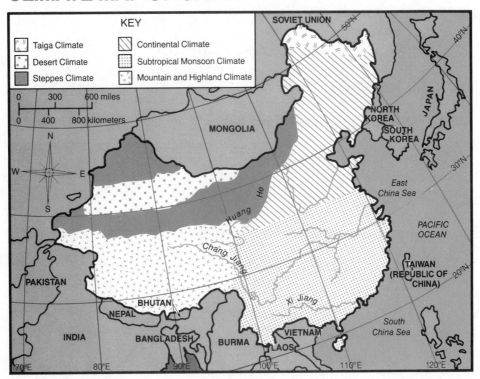

KEY

Taiga Climate   Continental Climate
Desert Climate   Subtropical Monsoon Climate
Steppes Climate   Mountain and Highland Climate

0   300   600 miles
0   400   800 kilometers

SOVIET UNION
MONGOLIA
NORTH KOREA
SOUTH KOREA
JAPAN
East China Sea
PACIFIC OCEAN
Huang He
Huang
Chang Jiang
Xi Jiang
TAIWAN (REPUBLIC OF CHINA)
South China Sea
PAKISTAN
BHUTAN
NEPAL
INDIA
BANGLADESH
BURMA
LAOS
VIETNAM

A. Finish the Sentence

Look at the climate map of China. Then write the word that finishes the sentence.

1. China has a taiga climate in part of the ▬.

   southeast   southwest   northeast

2. Most of the northeast has a ▬ climate.

   subtropical monsoon   steppes   continental

3. China has a desert climate in the ▬.

   northeast   southeast   west

4. China has mountains and highlands in the ▬.

   northeast   northwest   southwest

5. A ▬ climate has a hot, dry season for nine months and cold winters with a little rain.

   subtropical monsoon   steppes   continental

B. Write the Answer

Write a sentence to answer each question.

1. How do we use climate maps?

2. What is a continental climate like?

3. What is a subtropical monsoon climate like?

272

CHAPTER 37

China: A Communist Country

NEW WORDS: communes   Shanghai   uranium   bauxite
weapons   skilled workers   computers

Would you like to live in a country where every family
could have only one child? Today the leaders of China want
every family to be a one-child family.

   Why do the Chinese want to have one-child families? China
is a crowded country. Less than one fifth of the land is good
farm land. Today China grows most of the food it needs. Can
China grow enough food for many more people? Chinese
leaders do not think so. They want all families to have only
one child. Then there will be enough food for everyone. Today
most young families are having only one child.

Many Chinese farmers work on communes.

Chinese farmers are not allowed to own their land. Most food in China is grown on groups of farms called communes. The farmers share the work. All machines, tools, and animals are owned by the group. A member of the Communist party is the leader. The commune must give part of its crops to the government. Members share the rest of the crops with each other.

Most communes are very large. Some have more than 20,000 members. Schools and stores are part of the commune. Many have their own factories. There are villages too.

The communes have helped China grow enough food for its people. Today China grows more rice than any other country. China also grows a lot of wheat and corn.

Do the Chinese use modern ways of farming? On some communes, modern tools and machines are used. Fertilizer is also used. But on many communes, people and animals do most of the work.

Three fourths of China's people are farmers. Most Chinese people live in villages. More and more people are moving to China's cities. The country has many large cities. The city of Shanghai is one of the largest cities in the world. More than 12 million Chinese live in Shanghai.

China has many natural resources. There is a lot of oil. China has coal and iron. It has water power to make electricity. China has gold, silver, and tin. Uranium and bauxite are important minerals that are found in China.

China is a developing country. It is trying to become an industrial country. Many people now work in factories. For many years, Chinese factories made steel and weapons. They made farm machines and tools. But they made few consumer goods. Now Chinese factories are starting to make more consumer goods.

Today China trades with other countries. China sells goods to Japan, Hong Kong, and the United States. China also buys grain, machines, and fertilizers from other countries.

Transportation is a problem in China. People sail on rivers

and canals. There are good roads in the big cities. But many parts of China do not have many roads. The country does not have many railroads. It is hard to get from some parts of China to others.

China's leaders have many problems to solve. Their country has a great many people. The leaders want to

China is working to become an industrial country.

change China into an industrial country. But China does not have enough skilled, or trained, workers to be an industrial country. The country does not have many modern machines. It does not have many computers. Industrial countries need good transportation. The Chinese are trying to solve these problems. They want China to be a great world leader.

Think, Remember, Write

A. Locate the Answer

Write the correct answer to each question.

1. How many children do most young Chinese families have?

   1   7   5

2. What part of China's people are farmers?

   one fifth   one third   three fourths

3. Where do most Chinese live?

   in cities   in villages   in the desert

4. Which is China's largest city?

   Shanghai   Beijing   Calcutta

B. Find the Answer

On your paper, copy each sentence that tells about China. You should write 4 sentences.

1. Most food in China is grown on communes.

2. Commune members share the work and the crops.

3. Communes are owned by a few people.

4. The Chinese grow rice, wheat, and corn.

5. China is rich in diamonds.

6. China has iron, coal, and oil.

7. China's leaders want China to be a farming country.

C. Write It Right

The words in the sentences below are mixed up. Write each sentence correctly.

1. one fifth China's land of than Less farm land. is good

2. Communist party A member leader of the commune. of the is the

3. 20,000 members. Some communes more than have

4. more rice China grows any other country. than

5. gold, silver, bauxite, uranium, tin. and has China

6. with Japan, Hong Kong, United States. and the trades China

7. modern machines. computers many China have does not or

SKILL BUILDER 37: Reviewing Resource Maps

Skill Words

resource maps

Resource maps show where the natural resources of an area are found. Some resource maps show the factory goods of an area. Other resource maps show the farm goods of an area.

The map on the next page shows where natural resources are found in China. Steel is one of the metals on the map key. Steel itself is not a natural resource. It is a strong metal that is made from iron and coal. Industrial countries make a lot of steel.

The map shows that most of China's minerals are in eastern China. Most of China's people are in the east. Where do you think most Chinese factories can be found?

A. True or False

Write **T** for each sentence that is true. Write **F** for each sentence that is false.

1. The map shows that there are diamonds in China.

2. China has some oil and coal in the northwest.

3. There are steel factories in the northeast.

4. Iron and natural gas are found in the northeast.

5. Oil and coal are found near the Xi Jiang.

6. China has steel factories in the west.

7. There are steel factories near the Chang Jiang.

8. China has many natural resources in the southwest.

RESOURCE MAP OF CHINA

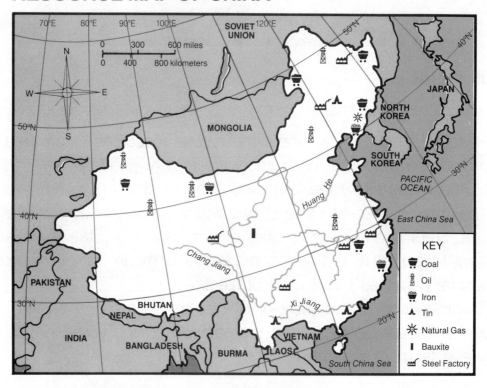

CHAPTER 38

Japan: An Archipelago Country

NEW WORDS: Japanese   archipelago   Honshu
Sea of Japan   Tokyo   televisions   traditions   bow
kimonos   Shinto   Buddhism   pollution

Is Japan a rich country or a poor country? Japan is very crowded. It has little farm land. It has few natural resources.

JAPAN

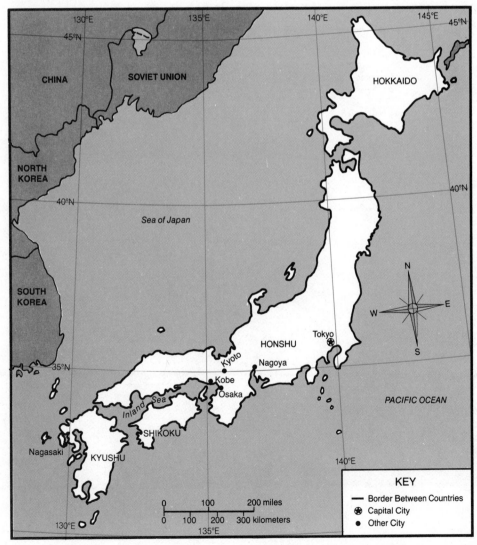

279

Sometimes there are dangerous earthquakes. Many people think these things would make Japan a poor country. But Japan is not poor. Japan is the richest country in Asia. In this chapter, you will learn why Japan is a rich country today.

The people of Japan are called Japanese. They speak the Japanese language. Their writing is a lot like Chinese writing. The Japanese use thousands of symbols to write their language.

Japan is an archipelago country. An archipelago is a group of islands. Japan has four large islands. It has hundreds of small islands. Honshu is the largest island. Most Japanese people live on Honshu.

The seas are important to Japan. The Japanese get a lot of their food from the sea. They eat a lot of fish. Japan uses the seas for shipping and trading. The seas also give Japan a good climate. The seas bring a lot of rain to Japan.

There is no place in Japan that is more than 100

Japan is a rugged island country.

miles *(160 kilometers)* from the sea. The Sea of Japan is to the west of the country. The Pacific Ocean is to the east.

Japan is a beautiful country. Large areas are covered with trees. Most of the land is covered with mountains. In Japan, people are always close to mountains.

Japan is a very crowded country. It has 120 million people. Most people live on plains near the coast. Few people live in the mountains.

Most Japanese live in cities. The largest city is Tokyo. It is Japan's capital. It is very crowded. It is one of the largest cities in the world.

Tokyo, Japan, is one of the largest cities in the world.

Only a small part of Japan's people are farmers. Less than one fifth of the land can be used for farming. Farms in Japan are small. The Japanese are very good farmers. They use modern tools and machines. They use lots of fertilizer. They grow huge amounts of food on their small farms. The

Japanese grow a lot of rice. Rice is the most important food in Japan. But the farmers do not grow enough food for all the people. Japan must import some of its food.

Japan has few natural resources. Its best resource is its people. They work very hard. They are skilled workers. Water power is another resource. Japan has wood from its trees. But the Japanese do not have oil, coal, or iron for their factories. They do not have many metals.

Japan is a great industrial country. The Japanese import oil and metals. They use them in their factories. The Japanese make more cars than any other country. They build more ships than any other country. The Japanese also make cameras and radios. They make televisions and computers. Japanese ships carry factory goods to many countries.

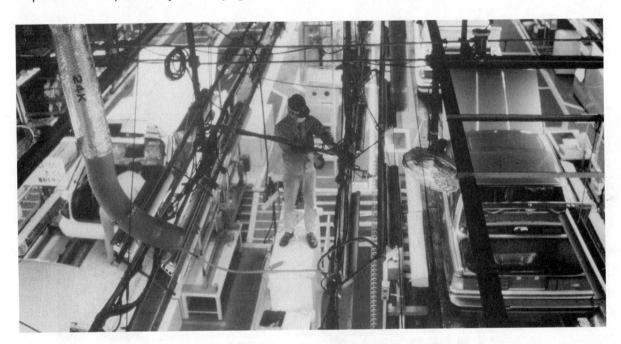

A car factory in Japan

Today Japan is a rich country. Japan makes more factory goods than any country in Western Europe. It is rich because it sells its goods to many countries of the world.

Japan is a strong democracy in Asia. Japan has its Parliament. People vote for their leaders. Japan's leader is the prime minister. Japan also has an emperor. He has little power.

Japan is a modern country. It has big cities. There is good transportation everywhere. Everyone knows how to read and write.

Japan is also a very old country. The Japanese love their old traditions. People bow to each other when they say hello and good-bye. People sometimes wear kimonos. These are beautiful Japanese robes. The Japanese always take off their shoes before going into a house. Many people believe in the Shinto or Buddhist religions.

Most people have a good life in Japan. But Japan has two big problems. It is very crowded. Pollution is another problem. Cars and factories are making the air and water very dirty.

Look around your home. Look at the cars in the street. You will see many goods from Japan. Today Japan is one of the world's great industrial countries.

Think, Remember, Write

A. Map Study

Look at the map of Japan on Page 279. Then finish each sentence in Group A with an answer from Group B. Write the letter of the correct answer on your paper.

Group A	Group B
1. An island in northern Japan is _____.	a. Honshu
2. An island in southern Japan is _____.	b. Sea of Japan
3. The largest island is _____.	c. Kyushu
4. The _____ is west of Japan.	d. Hokkaido
5. The _____ is east of Japan.	e. Pacific Ocean

B. Match Up

Finish each sentence in Group A with a word from Group B. Write the letter of the correct word on your paper.

<table>
<tr><td colspan="2" align="center">Group A</td><td align="center">Group B</td></tr>
<tr><td>1.</td><td>_____ is the richest country in Asia.</td><td>a. kimonos</td></tr>
<tr><td>2.</td><td>There is good _____ in Japan.</td><td>b. transportation</td></tr>
<tr><td>3.</td><td>_____ is Japan's capital.</td><td>c. mountains</td></tr>
<tr><td>4.</td><td>Japan makes more cars and _____ than any other country.</td><td>d. Shinto</td></tr>
<tr><td>5.</td><td>Beautiful Japanese robes are called _____</td><td>e. Honshu</td></tr>
<tr><td>6.</td><td>Most Japanese live on the island of _____</td><td>f. Japan</td></tr>
<tr><td>7.</td><td>Japan has a _____ problem from all of its cars and factories.</td><td>g. Tokyo</td></tr>
<tr><td>8.</td><td>Most of Japan is covered with _____</td><td>h. ships</td></tr>
<tr><td>9.</td><td>Buddhism and _____ are the religions of Japan.</td><td>i. archipelago</td></tr>
<tr><td>10.</td><td>An _____ is a group of islands.</td><td>j. pollution</td></tr>
</table>

C. True or False

Write **T** for each sentence that is true. Write **F** for each sentence that is false.

1. Japan has four large islands and hundreds of small ones.

2. Japanese farms are very large.

3. Japan is rich in natural resources.

4. Japan imports some of its food.

5. Japan is a democracy.

Skill Words

line graphs   decrease

Line graphs are used to show trends. These are changes that take place over time.

The line graph on this page shows the amount of money Japan has made by exporting cars. The graph shows the trend over the last 15 years. From the graph, we can learn that the amount of money grew sharply between 1975 and 1980. For one year, there was a decrease in the amount of money earned. This means less money was earned that year than the year before. But the trend for the years shown on the graph has been for the amount of money to grow.

MONEY JAPAN EARNED EXPORTING CARS

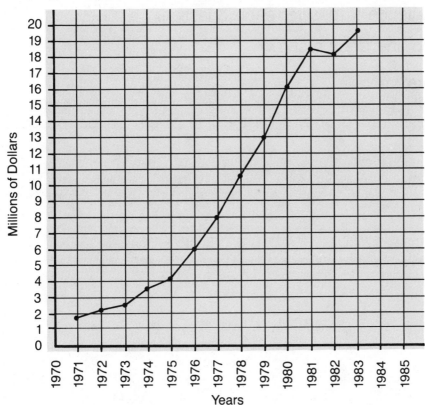

A. Finish Up

Look at the line graph. Then use the words in dark print to finish each sentence. Write the words you choose on your paper.

1982   **6**   **1971**   **19½**   **1983**

1. The least money was made in the year _____.

2. Japan made the most money in _____.

3. In 1976, _____ million dollars were made.

4. In 1983, _____ million dollars were made.

5. The only year that had a decrease in the amount of money was _____.

B. Write the Answer

Write a sentence to answer each question.

1. What do line graphs show?

2. What are trends?

3. What is the trend shown on the line graph on page 285?

CHAPTER 39

Australia: A Country and a Continent

NEW WORDS: kangaroos   reverse   reversed seasons
Great Dividing Range   Australians   Aborigines
Sydney   Canberra   Perth   sheep stations

Which country is also a continent? Which country has far more sheep than people? Which country is the home of many kinds of kangaroos? Australia is the answer.

AUSTRALIA

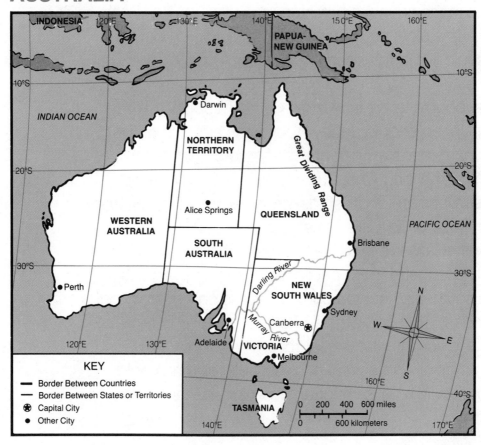

KEY
— Border Between Countries
— Border Between States or Territories
✪ Capital City
● Other City

Australia is the smallest continent. It is also the driest continent. Australia does not have very long rivers. Most of Australia gets little rain.

Australia is south of the Equator. It is in the Southern Hemisphere. The seasons there are the reverse of those in the Northern Hemisphere. When we have summer, Australia has winter. When we have winter, Australia has summer. What other countries are in the Southern Hemisphere? Those countries also have reversed seasons.

Northern Australia is in the tropics. The north is always hot. Most people live in the southeast. They live on coastal plains near the Pacific Ocean. This area gets plenty of rain. The climate is mild. Most of Australia's cities are there.

Australia has mountains that go north and south across the country. These mountains are called the Great Dividing Range. These mountains separate the coastal plains from the rest of the country. The huge land to the west of the Great Dividing Range gets little rain. Deserts cover one third of the country. Most of Australia's land has hills and plateaus. Few people live in the country's dry interior.

Australia is a big land with a small population. About 15 million people live in this country. The people are called Australians.

The first people to live in Australia were Aborigines. They are dark-skinned people. Today Aborigines are a small part of the country's people. They are often poorer than other Australians. For a long time, Australia was ruled by Britain. Many Australians are of British descent. English is the official language. Most people are Christians.

Most Australians live in cities. Sydney is the country's largest city. Canberra is the capital. Australia's largest cities are in the southeast near the coast. There is only one city on the west coast. That city is called Perth.

Australia is rich in natural resources. The country has coal and iron. It has oil and natural gas. Australia also has gold and diamonds. Mining is important to Australia. It exports many minerals.

Australia is an industrial country. Steel, machines, and clothing are a few things that are made in Australia. Most of the factory goods are used by the country's people. Most factory goods are not sold to other countries.

Only a small part of Australia's people are farmers. Australian farmers use modern ways of farming. They have good tools and machines. They grow more food than the country needs. Australia sells lots of wheat to other countries. The country exports other foods too.

Many places in the interior do not have enough rain for farming. But many areas have enough grass to raise sheep. The country has many sheep farms. The sheep farms are called sheep stations. Most stations are very large. Australians get meat and wool from their sheep. They export lots of wool. One third of the world's wool comes from Australia.

Australia has many large sheep stations.

Trade is important to Australia. Australia trades with Japan and the United States. It trades with New Zealand, Britain, and other countries.

Australia is a democracy. The country has its Parliament. People vote for their leaders. A prime minister is the country's leader. Australia belongs to the Commonwealth of Nations. All Commonwealth countries were once ruled by Britain.

Australia does face some problems today. There is pollution in the big cities. Cars and factories are making the air and water dirty. The country needs more irrigation. Dry land could be turned into good farm land. The country does not have good transportation everywhere. There is some in the large cities. But there are not many roads and railroads to join the country together.

Australia is a rich, modern country. Almost everyone knows how to read and write. The country has lots of food, factories, and raw materials. Most Australians believe their country is a very good place to live.

Think, Remember, Write

A. Finish Up

Use the words in dark print to finish each sentence. Write the words you choose on your paper.

**sheep   southeast   reversed seasons
Great Dividing Range   wool**

1. Australia has _____ because it is in the Southern Hemisphere.

2. Most Australians live in the _____

3. The mountains that separate the coastal plains from the rest of Australia are called the _____.

4. There are more _____ than people in Australia.

5. One third of the world's _____ comes from Australia.

B. Match Up

Finish each sentence in Group A with an answer from Group B. Write the letter of the correct answer on your paper.

Group A

1. There is plenty of rain in Australia's _____.

2. One third of Australia is _____.

3. The largest city in Australia is _____.

4. The capital of Australia is _____.

5. The only city on the west coast is _____.

Group B

a. Sydney

b. southeast

c. Perth

d. Canberra

e. desert land

C. Write the Answer

Write a sentence to answer each question.

1. Who were the first people to live in Australia?

2. What is Australia's official language?

3. What are six natural resources in Australia?

4. What are large sheep farms called?

5. What are some problems in Australia. Write 2 sentences.

Skill Words

pie chart   exports

You learned that a pie chart is a circle that has been divided into parts. All the parts form a whole circle.

Australia exports many goods. The pie chart shows you that there are three groups of exports. These three groups have all the goods Australia sells to other countries.

AUSTRALIAN EXPORTS

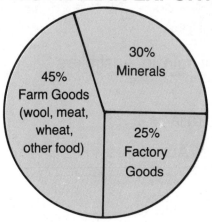

A. Finish Up

Look at the pie chart. Then use the words in dark print to finish each sentence. Write the words you choose on your paper.

smallest   25%   30%   farm goods   largest

1. Almost half of Australia's exports are _____.

2. Farm goods are the _____ group of exports.

3. Factory goods are the _____ group of exports.

4. Minerals are _____ of Australia's exports.

5. Factory goods are _____ of Australia's exports.

CHAPTER 40

The Future of East Asia and the Pacific

NEW WORDS: future   colony   borrowed   skills
depends   breathe

Most countries in East Asia and the Pacific want to be
part of the modern world. What are some of the problems
they face? How are the countries in this area working for their
future? The answers are in this chapter.

Workers in East Asia make goods for export all over the world.

Some countries have become Communist as a way to
solve their problems. China is one of these countries. China is

not the only Communist country in East Asia. After World War II, Korea became two countries. North Korea became a Communist country. South Korea is a non-Communist country.

Communist countries want more countries to have Communist governments. Most non-Communist countries want to remain free of Communist rule. North Korea would like South Korea to be a Communist state. Do you remember that Taiwan is a non-Communist country? Communist China would like to rule Taiwan.

Hong Kong is a small area to the south of China. It is a British colony. A colony is an area that is ruled by another country. In 1997 Britain will no longer rule Hong Kong. In that year, Communist China will take over Hong Kong. The struggle between Communist and non-Communist countries is a major problem of East Asia and the Pacific.

Hong Kong is a colony of Britain.

China, Japan, and Australia are the most important countries of this area. You have learned how they are trying to be modern, industrial countries. They now have new problems to solve.

What are some of China's new problems? China is trying to become an industrial country. It is a poor country. Its natural resources have not helped the Chinese people to live well. China does not have the money it needs to build new industries. It does not have enough skilled workers.

How is China solving these problems? The government runs all businesses. It has used a lot of its money to start new industries. China needs more money to become an industrial country. China has borrowed money from other countries. The government is allowing some other countries to build factories in China. They share the money they earn with China.

China is doing other things to become a modern country. China is buying computers from other countries. It is buying new machines. Some Chinese young people are studying in other countries. They are learning new skills. They will use them to help China become an industrial country.

Australia is a modern country. It is a rich country. Most people live well. But the population is small. Australia needs more people and more money to develop new industries. Australians want other countries to start businesses in Australia. Other countries can use their money to build mines and factories. They will share the money they earn with Australia.

Today Japan has the people and the money it needs to be an industrial country. But Japan needs raw materials. Japan imports its oil and minerals. Japan depends on other countries for its raw materials. In the years ahead, will Japan be able to buy all the oil, coal, and iron it needs? Without them, Japan cannot be an industrial country.

Many small countries in the Pacific are not yet part of the modern world. In these countries, most people are farmers. They often live and work the same way people did long ago. The people of these countries want to grow more food. They need to learn modern ways of farming.

Each year many countries of East Asia and the Pacific start new industries. Each year there are more cars on the streets of this area. The factories and cars are causing pollution. Most cities of this area have dirty air and water. It is not healthy to breathe dirty air. It is not healthy to drink dirty water. Pollution is not just a problem in East Asia and the Pacific. It is a problem in every industrial country in the world. In the years ahead, countries must work to find new ways of keeping their air and water clean.

Most people of East Asia and the Pacific have a better life than their parents had. Every day people around the world try to solve many kinds of problems. You have read about these problems in this book. Illiteracy, hunger, war, and pollution are a few of them. In every country, people are working for the future. Perhaps you too will work to build a better tomorrow for our world.

Think, Remember, Write

A. Find the Answer

On your paper, copy each sentence that tells about the countries of East Asia and the Pacific. You should write 3 sentences.

1. China, Japan, and Australia are trying to become modern, industrial countries.

2. Some Chinese young people are learning new skills by studying in other countries.

3. Japan has all the raw materials it needs.

4. Australia has enough people and money to develop new industries.

5. The people on the island countries of the Pacific need to learn modern ways of farming.

B. Match Up

Finish each sentence in Group A with an answer from Group B. Write the letter of the correct answer on your paper.

Group A	Group B
1. Many small countries in the Pacific must learn _____ ways to grow more food.	a. pollution
	b. depends
2. China does not have enough skilled _____ to be an industrial country.	c. modern
	d. develop
3. It is not healthy to _____ dirty air.	e. ruled
4. Cars and factories are causing _____ in every industrial country.	f. mines
	g. breathe
5. Japan _____ on other countries for raw materials for its factories.	h. workers
6. In 1997 Hong Kong will be _____ by Communist China.	i. borrowed
7. Australia wants other countries to _____ its mines.	j. colony
8. Hong Kong is a British _____.	
9. China has _____ money from other countries to start new factories.	
10. Australia has many metals and minerals in its _____.	

C. Write It Right

The words in the sentences below are mixed up. Write each sentence correctly.

1. non-Communist countries Most remain rule. of Communist want to free

2. another country. colony A ruled by is that is an area

3. more people and more money Australia needs new industries. to develop

4. the problems of illiteracy, hunger, war, pollution. and People trying to solve are

SKILL BUILDER 40: Reviewing Bar Graphs

Skill Words

bar graphs   Pyongyang   Seoul

Bar graphs are used to compare facts. They can also help you learn information quickly.

The bar graph on the next page compares the number of people in five large cities in East Asia and the Pacific. One of these cities is Pyongyang. It is the capital of North Korea. Seoul is also shown. It is the capital of South Korea. The graph shows us that Pyongyang has the smallest population of the five cities. It is easy to see that Shanghai is the largest city.

A. Finish the Sentence

Look at the bar graph. Then write the word that finishes the sentence.

1. Shanghai has almost === million people.

   5   10   12

2. Seoul has almost the same population as ══.

Tokyo   Sydney   Shanghai

3. The population of Tokyo is more than ══ million.

4   8   10

4. The population of Sydney is more than ══ million.

1   2   3

5. The population of Pyongyang is a little more than ══ million.

1   2   3

POPULATIONS OF FIVE CITIES

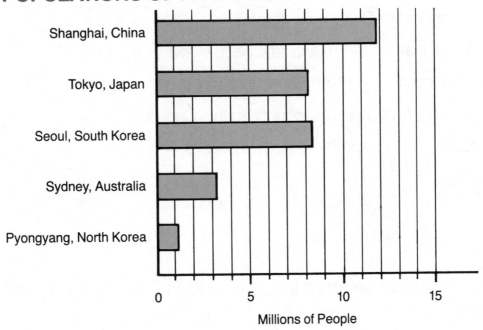

Millions of People

REVIEW 1 • CHAPTERS 1– 5

A. Finish the Sentence

Write the word that finishes the sentence.

1. The United States and Canada are industrial countries because they have many ▬▬▬.

   forests   rivers   factories

2. The United States has ▬▬▬ states.

   10   50   100

3. The government of the United States is in ▬▬▬.

   Washington, D.C.   Toronto   Montreal

4. More than half of Canada's people live in the ▬▬▬.

   cold north   Canadian Shield   St. Lawrence Lowlands

5. American companies control many Canadian ▬▬▬.

   farms   airports   businesses

B. True or False

Write **T** for each sentence that is true. Write **F** for each sentence that is false.

1. The United States and Canada have the same flag, money, and leaders.

2. Puerto Rico is an island that belongs to the United States.

3. Every year people from many countries come to live in the United States and Canada.

4. Canada is a democracy today.

5. Some French Canadians want the province of Quebec to be a free French country.

300

REVIEW 2 • CHAPTERS 6–10

A. Locate the Answer

Write the correct answer to each question.

1. The first Europeans in Latin America came from what countries?

   England and Spain   Portugal and France

   Portugal and Spain

2. Where do most Mexicans live?

   the Central Plateau   the mountains   Acapulco

3. Where do village people buy and sell goods in Latin America?

   at the market   on their farms   in apartment houses

4. Where do most Brazilians live?

   the interior   the northeast   the south near the ocean

5. Where in Latin America is illiteracy a big problem?

   Argentina   Costa Rica   Haiti

B. Match Up

Finish each sentence in Group A with an answer from Group B. Write the letter of the correct answer on your paper.

Group A	Group B
1. People who are of Spanish and Indian descent are called	a. Portugal
2. The water to the east of Mexico is called	b. mestizos
3. Mexico sells most of its goods to	c. the United States
4. Brazil was settled by people from	d. Costa Rica
5. Most people in Argentina and ...... can read and write.	e. the Gulf of Mexico

REVIEW 3 • CHAPTERS 11–15

A. Finish the Sentence

Write the word that finishes the sentence.

1. The waters of the Atlantic Ocean keep the land of Europe ===.

   too cold   warm   too hot

2. England, Scotland, and === are the three parts of Britain.

   Wales   Sweden   Italy

3. === is a country with snow-covered mountains and beaches on the Mediterranean Sea.

   Britain   France   West Germany

4. The country that exports the most factory goods in Western Europe is ===.

   Britain   France   West Germany

5. The countries of Western Europe are joined together by ===.

   transportation   language   religion

B. True or False

Write **T** for each sentence that is true. Write **F** for each sentence that is false.

1. Western Europe is a large peninsula with a long coast.

2. Britain's queen makes all of Britain's laws.

3. France is the largest country in Western Europe.

4. West Germany grows more food than any other country in Western Europe.

5. Common Market members must pay tariffs on goods that they buy and sell from each other.

REVIEW 4 • CHAPTERS 16–20

A. Locate the Answer

Write the correct answer to each question.

1. Who owns most farms, factories, stores, and businesses in Communist countries?

   farmers   workers   the government

2. Which mountains separate the European part of the Soviet Union from the Asian part of the country?

   Andes   Urals   Alps

3. What does the Soviet Union buy from the United States?

   wheat   oil   trees

4. Which Communist country has privately owned farms?

   East Germany   Hungary   Poland

B. Finish Up

Use the words in dark print to finish each sentence. Write the words you choose on your paper.

freedom   trade unions   Moscow   Warsaw Pact   weapons

1. Most factories of Communist countries make steel and _____.

2. Soviet leaders in _____ make all important laws for the Soviet Union.

3. The people of the Soviet Union do not have the _____ to speak or write against the government.

4. The Poles tried to start free _____ that were not controlled by the Communist party.

5. In 1956 soldiers from countries in the _____ fought along with the Soviets against the people of Hungary.

REVIEW 5 • CHAPTERS 21-25

A. True or False

Write **T** for each sentence that is true. Write **F** for each sentence that is false.

1. Some countries in the Middle East and North Africa are rich in oil.

2. Few people in Egypt live near the Nile River.

3. Israel sells oil and natural resources to other countries.

4. Saudi Arabia is a rich country because it has a lot of oil.

5. Lack of peace is a big problem in the Middle East and North Africa.

B. Match Up

Finish each sentence in Group A with an answer from Group B. Write the letter of the correct answer on your paper.

Group A	Group B
1. Two Muslim countries in the Middle East that are not Arab countries are	a. oranges, grapefruit, and flowers
2. The Aswan High Dam has given Egypt a lot more	b. Syria
3. Israel exports	c. desalting plants
4. The country of .... has been a leader in the wars against Israel.	d. Turkey and Iran
5. The countries of this area should build .... to get more fresh water.	e. farm land

REVIEW 6 • CHAPTERS 26-30

A. Finish Up

Use the words in dark print to finish each sentence. Write the words you choose on your paper.

Apartheid   **oil**
highlands   **cash crops**

1. Coffee, tea, cocoa, and palm oil are some of Africa's _____.

2. Nigeria earns most of its money from its _____ industry.

3. Most of Kenya's people live in the southwest _____.

4. _____ laws keep the four groups of South Africans apart.

B. Locate the Answer

Write the correct answer to each question.

1. Where is most of Africa?

   in the Arctic   in the Western Hemisphere   in the tropics

2. Which African country has the most people?

   Kenya   Nigeria   South Africa

3. Which African country earns money from exporting coffee?

   Kenya   Nigeria   South Africa

4. Which African country is rich in gold and diamonds?

   Kenya   Nigeria   South Africa

REVIEW 7 • CHAPTERS 31-34

A. Finish the Sentence

Write the word that finishes the sentence.

1. The most important food in South and Southeast Asia is ══.

   wheat   corn   rice

2. Most of India's food is grown on the ══.

   fertile plain   Deccan Plateau   Himalaya Mountains

3. The government of India is working to end the ══.

   religion   caste system   schools

4. In many places, Indian farmers are using ══ to yield better crops.

   miracle seeds   new roads   new schools

5. A non-Communist country in Southeast Asia is ══.

   Vietnam   Kampuchea   Thailand

B. True or False

Write **T** for each sentence that is true. Write **F** for each sentence that is false.

1. Most countries in South and Southeast Asia have many factories and industries.

2. The monsoon winds bring rain to most countries in South and Southeast Asia.

3. India gets monsoon rains from June to September.

4. India is never able to export grain.

5. There is peace in South and Southeast Asia today.

REVIEW 8 • CHAPTERS 35-40

A. Locate the Answer

Write the correct answer to each question.

1. Which country is **not** an industrial country?

   Australia   Japan   China

2. Where do people use bicycles instead of cars?

   China   Japan   Australia

3. Which country makes the most cars and ships?

   China   Japan   Australia

4. Which country is a continent?

   Australia   New Zealand   Taiwan

5. Which country depends on other countries for raw materials for its factories?

   China   Japan   Australia

B. Match Up

Finish each sentence in Group A with an answer from Group B. Write the letter of the correct answer on your paper.

Group A	Group B
1. Most people are farmers on	a. food and raw materials
2. The leader of the Communist party is the leader of	b. Communist countries
3. The Japanese import	c. the small islands of Oceania
4. Australia and other countries in the Southern Hemisphere have	d. China
5. Taiwan and South Korea do not want to be	e. reversed seasons

FINAL REVIEW PART 1: UNITED STATES, CANADA, LATIN AMERICA, AND EUROPE

Finish the Sentence

Write the word that finishes the sentence.

1. ═══ is the second largest country in the world.

   the Soviet Union   England   Canada

2. The ═══ is a large river in the United States.

   Mississippi   St. Lawrence   Amazon

3. The first people to live in the United States were the ═══.

   English   Indians   Spanish

4. ═══ is grown on the Great Plains of the United States and Canada and is used to make bread.

   rice   wheat   bananas

5. Almost one third of the people of Canada are ═══.

   Spanish   Mexican   French

6. The tall mountains of South America are called the ═══.

   Alps   Urals   Andes

7. The official language of Mexico is ═══.

   Portuguese   French   Spanish

8. A country where tourists go to its beaches during the winter months is ═══.

   Canada   Mexico   England

9. The largest country of Latin America is ═══.

   Mexico   Argentina   Brazil

10. A country that grows a lot of coffee is ═══.

    France   Canada   Colombia

308

11. No place in ▬▬ is more than 300 miles *(480 kilometers)* from the sea.

    Western Europe   South America   the Soviet Union

12. ▬▬ is a country where laws are made in Parliament.

    the United States   Britain   Brazil

13. ▬▬ is a country that touches the North Sea, Atlantic Ocean, and Mediterranean Sea.

    Canada   Mexico   France

14. ▬▬ was divided and became two countries after World War II.

    England   Germany   France

15. The United States, Canada, and the Western European countries of ▬▬ have promised to fight for each other during a war.

    the Common Market   the Commonwealth of Nations   NATO

16. Farms that are owned by the government in the Soviet Union are called ▬▬.

    state farms   provinces   one-crop economies

17. Almost half of the Soviet Union is covered with ▬▬.

    deserts   frozen land   beaches

18. ▬▬ is ruled by its Communist party.

    Canada   Britain   the Soviet Union

19. ▬▬ is a Communist country where most people practice the Roman Catholic religion.

    Poland   the Soviet Union   East Germany

20. The six countries of Eastern Europe known as satellites obey ▬▬.

    the Soviet Union   the United States   Yugoslavia

FINAL REVIEW PART 2: AFRICA, ASIA, AUSTRALIA, AND THE MIDDLE EAST

Finish the Sentence

Write the word that finishes the sentence.

1. The Sahara covers much of ▭.

    South Africa   North Africa   China

2. The official language of Egypt is ▭.

    Spanish   French   Arabic

3. ▭ is Israel's capital, and it is a city with many holy places.

    Cairo   Tokyo   Jerusalem

4. Islam teaches that every Muslim must try to visit the city of ▭.

    Mecca   Jerusalem   Damascus

5. There is a large desalting plant in ▭.

    Saudi Arabia   Egypt   Kuwait

6. Many metals are found in mines in ▭.

    the Middle East   Africa   Japan

7. An African country that is rich in oil is ▭.

    Nigeria   Kenya   South Africa

8. Kenya is in eastern Africa near the ▭ Ocean.

    Atlantic   Indian   Arctic

9. The richest country in Africa is ▭.

    Egypt   Kenya   South Africa

10. Illiteracy, poverty, and ▭ are some of Africa's problems.

    religion   mountains   sickness

11. The monsoon winds bring lots of rain to ▭.

    the Middle East   South and Southeast Asia   South Africa

12. India has the largest ══ system in Asia.

    railroad   factory   irrigation

13. The Green Revolution is helping Indians get more ══.

    transportation   food   factories

14. South and Southeast Asia has had many ══.

    wars   cities   teachers

15. The islands of the ══ and Australia are called Oceania.

    Pacific   Atlantic   United States

16. The country with more than one billion people is ══.

    Kenya   China   Australia

17. Most people in China are ══.

    factory workers   farmers   doctors

18. One of the world's great industrial countries is ══.

    Thailand   Nigeria   Japan

19. A big country with a small population is ══.

    Australia   Taiwan   South Africa

20. The factories and cars in industrial countries are causing ══

    hunger   pollution   illiteracy

Total Vocabulary List

All the new words of **World Geography and You** are listed below. The number next to each word shows the chapter where you first read the word.

A

Aborigines	39
Acapulco	7
acid rain	5
adults	8
Africa	3
Afrikaans	29
agriculture	10
airlines	5
Alaska	2
Albania	16
Alps	11
Amazon River	6
American Indians	3
Americans	2
Anatolia	25
Andes Mountains	6
Antarctica	6
apartheid	29
apartment houses	8
Arabic	21
Arabs	21
archipelago	38
Arctic Ocean	4
Argentina	10
armies	25
Asia	6
Asians	11
assume	35
Aswan High Dam	22
Atlantic Ocean	2
Australia	35
Australians	39

B

Baltic Sea	19
Bangkok	34
Bangladesh	31
bar graphs	15
bauxite	37
Bedouins	21
Beijing	36
Benares	33
Berlin	14

bicycle	35
billion	36
Black Sea	17
Bonn	14
border	1
borders	16
borrowed	40
bow	38
Brahmaputra River	32
Brasília	9
Brazil	6
Brazilians	9
breathe	40
Britain	12
British Isles	12
Buddhism	38
Buddhists	31

C

Cairo	22
Calcutta	32
California	2
camera	35
Canada	1
Canadians	1
Canadian Shield	4
canals	13
Canberra	39
capital	9
Caribbean Sea	6
cash crops	26
Caspian Sea	17
caste	33
caste system	33
cattle	9
Caucasians	11
centimeters	19
central	25
Central America	6
Central Plateau	7
chancellor	14
Chang Jiang	36
chemicals	5
China	35
Chinese	36

Christian	22
churches	18
climate	11
climate map	23
coal	3
coast	11
coastal plains	28
cocoa	26
coconut	34
collectives	16
college	30
Colombia	10
colony	40
Coloreds	29
column	9
Comecon	20
Common Market	15
Commonwealth of Nations	12
communes	37
Communist party	16
Communists	16
companies	5
compare	15
compass rose	3
computers	37
consumer goods	16
continental	36
continents	6
control	5
copper	21
corn	30
Corsica	13
Costa Rica	10
costly	23
crops	8
culture	26
Czechoslovakia	19

D

dam	22
Damascus	24
Dead Sea	23
Deccan Plateau	32
decrease	38
degrees	12